ORGANIZATIONAL VIOLENCE

ORGANIZATIONAL VIOLENCE

Creating a Prescription for Change

Lloyd C. Williams

QUORUM BOOKS
Westport, Connecticut • London

Library of Congress Cataloging-in-Publication Data

Williams, Lloyd C.
   Organizational violence : creating a prescription for change /
Lloyd C. Williams.
      p.   cm.
   Includes bibliographical references and index.
   ISBN 0–89930–808–2 (alk. paper)
   1. Violence.   2. Organizational change.   3. Organizational
sociology.   I. Title.
HM281.W53   1994
303.6—dc20   93–27711

British Library Cataloguing in Publication Data is available.

Library of Congress Catalog Card Number: 93–27711
ISBN: 0–89930–808–2

First published in 1994

Quorum Books, 88 Post Road West, Westport, CT 06881
An imprint of Greenwood Publishing Group, Inc.

Printed in the United States of America

The paper used in this book complies with the
Permanent Paper Standard issued by the National
Information Standards Organization (Z39.48–1984).

10 9 8 7 6 5 4 3 2 1

This book is dedicated to all of my clients—
past, present, and future

Contents

Tables and Figures

Preface

This book is the second consecutive book of mine that looks at the creation of congruence and balance. *Organizational Violence* is based on the challenges I have experienced working with governments and private corporations as a change agent for fifteen years. Jack Gibb, Will McWhinney, Frank Friedlander, Charlie Seashore, Christine Ho, and Mark Hickson have been crucial in guiding my thinking for the creation of this theory. Managers and public executives have been critical in helping me to live the experience of the violence paradigm, and my clients have helped change organizational histories that foster violence. My clients have also provided the continual challenge to my thinking and have helped me crystallize the creation of my theory of violence. I thank all of my clients for utilizing my system of change and my co-consultants in Change Management Resources for challenging my process of change, demanding that I clarify, clarify, clarify. I sincerely wish to express my deepest gratitude to Anthony "Tony" Gebarowski for helping me design the figures and tables used in this book and for his assistance in technically restructuring the book.

Finally, I want to thank the City of Las Vegas organization for taking the risk of embracing my system of expunging organizational violence. You have been a challenge; yet, like children, you have a thirst for growing and changing. For that, I will always treasure the collaboration and the outcomes.

Introduction

During the past fifty years, management and organizational theorists have postured that organizations change because of a stimulus that impacts either the bottom line or the overall strategies that have guided the work and the decision-making process of their organizations. Throughout this period, an underlying seed of dissension has grown that often gets overlooked by the decision makers, the managers, and the theorists.

The process of creating change is often wrought with trauma, pain, a sense of loss, or out-of-control actions. The conventional wisdom has discounted the underlying dissension as jealousy, misunderstanding, or sabotage on the part of competitors. This process of *discounting* typifies the situation that caused me to write this book. As a public manager, organizational development and organizational change consultant, sometimes clinical therapist, and a person of color who has often struggled to create a level of balance in my life, I have always been struck by the reactions one experiences when acting as the bearer of "bad news." More than not, the reactions seem to far outweigh the situation at hand. Upon review of the varying reactions, I began to identify key issues that impacted the successful exchange of information from one person to another. From a consulting perspective, I have watched organizations make sound, ethical decisions but implement those decisions in very unsound ways. From a public manager's perspective, I have watched organizational executives make decisions that appear to "half-step" what needs to occur in order for the actions to be worthwhile. As a father, I have watched my two sons respond differently to situations, wondering why the reactions seem so out of balance. As a life partner, I have watched historical tapes—that is, memories that cause pain—guide reactions that seem off kilter to the situation, and have wondered what the underlying cause of the reactions could be. What began to emerge in my thinking was the underlying issue of violence, both personal and organizational. This book looks at the issue of violence and the elements of a violence paradigm that impact the successful maintenance and movement of organizational systems from one span of history to another.

Throughout history, society has embraced the concept of violence as a means to achieve ends deemed valuable for the perceived greater good of the community. During the Salem witch hunts, the Spanish Inquisition, periods of slavery, the Civil War, and other historic battles, violence was deemed good and appropriate for society. Violence was legitimated by the church and carried out by its protectors. Violence was in tune with the church and the American way, if violence met the needs and was for the benefit of the larger group.

Violence is the unjust, callous, emotionally disturbed, and sometimes explosive use of power or force to alter the true form of an idea, ideal, plan, or action. Violence is a violation of ethics in its attempt to alter the intrinsic values or good of an idea, policy, or practice. Violence is a tool of organizations and a purveyor of tensions among philosophy, policy, and practice; and only through an examination of the violations of sound philosophy, policy, and practice can a commitment to expunging violence be understood, much less put into action.

This book assesses the process of organizational violence. Organizations avoid making sound decisions through a continual process of narrowing and controlling choices. In the narrowing of choice, trauma is created organizationally, and people and the organization suffer. In the controlling of choice, organizations establish a framework to blame the challenger or sabotage the change process. To feel whole, people and organizations often rationalize their behavior through a process of discounting, empowerment, exclusion, and nonbonding. What is often not understood is the real outcome of the utilization of violence.

Part one of this book looks at the unhealthy development of organizational violence. I assert that the creation of violence is often a covert act without malice; yet the outcome becomes a malicious process. The case is made for the existence of a system of violence and its utilizations within organizational life.

Part two is comprised of four cases depicting organizational violence. The first chapter is about the Southwest Medical Research Center dictating change within its organization as an attempt to build congruence. The case looks at the outcomes accomplished by the organization and the damages created. The second chapter focuses on the downsizing of city government. Central City believed it was responding to clear direction and downsized in a caring manner; yet the process produced an enormous violent reaction. The third chapter focuses on Northeast Test Preparation Center, which brought in a new crop of MBA's to manage the corporation. The new leaders instituted a change process that to this day leaves a bad taste in the mouths of the recipients of the change. The fourth chapter looks at cultural change within a county government and the impacts the change had on the employees and managers. This last case is critical because it identifies how success can be achieved with traditional management approaches, but the success is short-lived because of underlying violence issues.

Part three is the heart of the theory. Critical to the expunging of violence is recognizing the placement of violence and the process of movement within violence. This is critical, for it challenges all management theories that discount the existence of a violence paradigm. This part focuses on understanding the violence paradigm, creation of a nonviolence paradigm, and how balance and movement occur in effective ways.

The thrust of this book is that balance and movement are often thwarted, creating a violence cycle that is hard to expunge. Embracing comprehensiveness is critical to organizational success. Embracing and creating balance is critical to wholeness. It is a book of building awareness, recognizing wholeness, and revisiting and repairing one's history, personally and organizationally.

Part One

The Structure of Violence

1

============

A Perspective on
Organizational Violence

During the 1980s and into the 1990s, a plethora of lawsuits have occurred focusing on organizations' treatment of their employees. The traditional view has been to chastise attorneys for creating unnecessary lawsuits. Organizations have indicated that "they have done nothing wrong," yet they have been penalized for decisions that have allowed them to remain in business and remain competitive. Labor unions have complained that management has been consistently unfair in the treatment of employees, first agreeing to contractual language then creating avenues to usurp the language under the guise of tightening budget revenues. Minorities have worked hard to break organizational "glass ceilings" to no avail, often being passed over for promotions while training their new superiors. Women contended during the 1992 election process that white males have continually discriminated against and abused women, leading them to become more feminist and politically active by electing women to political office. Riots broke out in Los Angeles and other cities in 1992 as a reaction to years of economic, educational, and racial neglect. Each of these situations is a form of organizational and institutional violence.

Throughout history, society has embraced violence as a way of achieving ends deemed valuable for the perceived greater good of the community. There is a problem with this historical embracing of violence, and that problem is the sustaining of an unethical choice to achieve a desired outcome.

Lawyers define violence as the unlawful use of force. This definition leaves a lot to be desired. The oppressed person or organization might say that society creates violence as a method of controlling and exploiting the powerless, the poor, the uneducated, and the minority. Sociologists might define violence as the inappropriate utilization of power by the authority of a society such as police, lawyers, church leaders, or politicians. A socialist might say that social orders other than socialism are innately violent in utilization of societal controllers—police, army, courts, prisons—to maintain positions and privileges of the middle and upper classes. Ethnic groups might define violence as the practice of exclusion by the majority classes of groups of ethnic minorities in keeping minorities from participating in and benefiting from the rewards and rituals of society. Still others might describe violence as the deliberate act of the white male majority to pit all nonwhite males against one another in competition for a very small piece of the societal pie. Examples of this form of violence might be the creation of ghettos or racist, segregated educational and social organizations.

Governments and corporations look at the issue of organizational violence differently. *Violence* is often too harsh a term for them to embrace. Governments speak of changes in policies as a reflection of the "will" of the people in their desire for quality-of-life enhancements. Often the process of enhancing the quality of life requires altering approaches to public service and service delivery. Governments would state that unions are unwilling to traverse the waters of change and present obstacles to policy shifts. When dealing with violence, corporations speak of the necessity to alter the manner of business conduct. They challenge that changes made are unethical, stating that the desired outcome—responsibility to the investors—often demands radical changes in process and procedure. Employees are not looking out for the company, only for themselves. Therefore, if violence or dissatisfaction is the perspective of the employee, the directors of corporations must take the larger view, the high road, to ensure the success and viability of the organization. In other words, based on their lack of ability to "call a spade a spade," organizations rationalize their destructive behaviors in terms of policy shifts, quality shifts, and appropriate business conduct.

Violent and oppressive social and organizational systems evolve over a long period of time. The originators of these violent systems have long since passed from our existence; however, the benefactors of these violent systems continue today to foster oppressive environments. Systems, not individuals, are the oppressors of violent organizations. Systems, as well as organizational and legislative practices, are also the current purveyors of organizational injustice within our society. Since violence is a violation of ethics, which attempts to alter the intrinsic value or good of an idea, policy, or practice, only through an examination and commitment to ethical decision making can the cycle of violence within organizations be rechanneled.

This book assesses the process of organizational violence. As stated previously, organizations avoid ethical decision making through a continual process of narrowing choices, which creates trauma. To feel whole, people and organizations often rationalize their violent behavior through a paradoxical question: Is it better to bend or corrupt the rules and solve all the problems within organizational life, or is an ethically solid organization that adheres to the rules yet fails in solving problems and issues more valid? The answer is often to embrace the corrupt organizational process.

In a one-week period during May 1992, the *Los Angeles Times* contained several articles questioning ethical choice and the potential for "organizational and institutional violence." The articles include:

"House Post Office Probe to Include Rostenkowski"

"U.S. Probes Payments at Seized Bank"

"Cranston and Seymour Lack Clout, Colleagues Say: Democrat's Ethics Problems Hinder Them, Critics Contend"

"Doctor Barred from Practicing Pending Hearing: Accused of Performing Unnecessary Eye Surgeries"

"Keating Kin Makes Deal with Feds"

"Son-in-Law Pleads Guilty to Misapplying $14 Million in Deposits"

"McDonnell Aid Efforts Criticized: A Pentagon Investigator Says the Air Force's Plan May Have Violated the Law"

"Marketers Rethinking Violent Ads"

"United Way Scandal Puts New Focus on Nonprofit Pay Levels"

"Two Fired for Staying Home During Violence: Centinel Hospital Medical Center Defends Its Personnel Policies"

Each of these articles addresses impropriety on the part of persons and organizations that traumatized and violated an idea, policy, or practice.

There are numerous avenues one can use to approach the subject of organizational violence. These avenues can be based on assessing the number of violent acts that occur within organizations, shootings of employees, leveraged buy out situations, union strikes, reductions in force, and so on. However, assessing organizational violence based on the acts misses the underlying issues that create these various acts. In each situation, some change has occurred through the policies or practices of the organization. The issue of violence becomes a response or reaction to an unexpected, unexplained, unwarranted change in a policy, procedure, or practice that creates trauma among employees and in the organization itself. Therefore, what is helpful in exploring organizational violence is assessing the tenets of violence.

TENETS OF VIOLENCE

Violence is both a personal and organizational intrusion into society. Violence is created because of the absence of key components in the developmental process of people and organizational systems. These key factors are:

1. the ability of people and organizations to effectively create bonds that foster collaboration and inclusiveness;
2. placing a high value on inclusiveness in sharing among people the process of growth and understanding regarding the desired outcomes of organizations;
3. balancing the need for individuality with the work ethic of team performance;
4. embracing rather than discounting the introduction of ideas and ideals;
5. resolving issues of control, power, and authority; and
6. assessing life's dichotomies where choices are made, regarding ends justifying the means versus the means being a critical dynamic toward achieving an appropriate and just end.

In evaluating organizational performance, organizations must realize that success goes beyond the completion of a project. Organizational success must be balanced by assessing the health of the employees and the organizational congruence of policies, procedures, and practices along with the outcomes of any projects. Fiscal health and success must be balanced with adherence to organizational ideals. Successful growth and development can only be long term when policies and goals mirror the actions of an organization's officers toward a given end.

In Bryan Burrough's book *Vendetta: American Express and the Smearing of Edmond Safra* (New York: HarperCollins, 1992), President/CEO Jim Robinson is reported to have said, "Integrity is fundamental to every business we're in" (p. 59). Ethical policy and ethical behavior are fundamental to every business—private, public, and nonprofit. Without the ethical perspective, organizational violence can become the norm for action.

Bonding versus Nonbonding

Andy Anaheim was a fictional character once utilized by the city of Anaheim, California, to introduce new employees to the city. Andy Anaheim was a character who talked about the mission of service to the citizens of the city. Employees were acquainted with the work ethic, city history, services provided, and benefits given for quality customer/citizen service during one's employment with the organization. Disneyland, in Anaheim, also maintains a fictional character to acquaint employees with the Disneyland ethos and look. These two characters represent the initial approach of a government and private corporation to the concept of bonding. Bonding is a joining of an organization with an individual to build a relationship. It describes the parameters of the relationship to include caring about, comfort with, closeness to, respect for, and integrity for each other. The relationship is continued through the organization's commitment to enhance the employees' ability to be successful. This process usually involves training, educational opportunities, cross-training opportunities, and promotions as evidence that the organization cares about the success of its employees and values its relationship with the employees.

Too often, employees describe a nonbonding relationship with their employer. The nonbonding process involves deceit, noncommitment, abandonment, and disrespect on the part of the organization toward the employee. The resulting outcome of the behavior is mistrust, fear-oriented behavior, and a divesting of faith and commitment to the organization, by the employees. Organizations state that no disrespect is intended but that a change in priorities occurs demanding a shifting of vital resources. Unfortunately, employees do not believe this. Sometimes organizations state that employees should grow with the organization, implying for many employees a marriage of sorts, that is, that monogamy and fidelity to the organization bring certain rewards and gains. However, employees too often find themselves divorced from their organizational spouse and sense that the relationship is indeed not a marriage but an affair. The outcome, again, is one of disbelief, hurt, pain, and trauma whether the relationship is a three-month or a twenty-year experience. This is a process of nonbonding. Economic coverage by any of the television news media displays employees in dismay and disbelief regarding an organization's treatment of them in mergers, leveraged buy outs, plant closings, or reductions in force.

The issue of bonding represents the approach all persons learn in forging lasting and effective relationships in life. The process begins at birth, with the child bonding with the mother and/or father. The degree to which a child receives nurturing from his or her parents or other care givers determines the calmness and ability of the child to respond rather than react to stress and pain. The same dynamic is true within organizations. An organization's nurturing of the employee enhances the employee's ability to be flexible with changes in organizational life. Not to nurture defeats the organization's need to have the employee's commitment to the organization. Not to bond creates an unhealthy and unnatural tendency to become self-oriented and unable to participate in the process of sharing and collaborating. The process of nonbonding becomes an act of violence. The extreme is antisocial, borderline personality issues. For example, a lifelong employee has given his or her life to the corporation, and the corporation merges with another, robbing the pension fund, laying off the employee, and disrupting the potential of the employee to maintain his or her sense of liberty. There is a struggle of balance between relationships with employees and the profitability of the shareholders of the organization. The cycle of violence begins when the employee is devalued. The cycle of violence continues as valuing things over people is deemed acceptable.

Inclusion versus Exclusion

When I was nine years old, I joined a Little League baseball team. My pitching was satisfactory, but not great. The coach was respectful of me and worked with me on a daily basis to improve my skills. The team was less kind. I was hounded because I was not a great pitcher and taunted for every mistake that I made. I had been excluded from the group; the experience was horrible. I never forgot that experience, and later in life I have worked hard to ensure that all of my employees have been included as much as possible in the actions of the organizations for which I have worked. However, my experience as a ball player matches the experience of an astounding number of employees in the work environment. Where organizations are good at bonding, often they are lousy at inclusiveness. Many organizations have spent little time practicing an *inclusive organizational lifestyle*. Organizational policy needs to identify the value that the organization maintains, respecting diversity and collaboration as means to a just and appropriate end in the goals identified within the organization. For example, employees on the job need to feel included in selecting fellow workers who must join their team.

There are various aspects of the inclusion-exclusion dichotomy. Employees feel excluded when they begin to retreat into their own world in order to protect themselves. Employees feel included when they embrace the concepts of diversity, newness, and change within the organization. Employees also feel excluded when they begin to suspect the organization's intentions to care about their well-being. In some cases, a lack of inclusiveness gives way to creating assumptions regarding the organization's actions. Unfortunately, when this thinking heightens to the point of fear, employees tend to take a skewed view of any action by the organization. This alteration of views begins to deter the organization from achieving its desired outcomes. The organization begins to experience heightened union activity; increased accidents, raising risk management costs; and increased sick leave usage, causing increased health costs and management issues. The more a person or group of persons feels excluded, the more the validation and perception of organizational violence grow. The more organizations rationalize their actions of exclusion, the angrier persons on the periphery become, believing that the actions of the organization are deliberate and unjust.

Balancing Individuality and Team Performance

Employees have learned that, in our society, individual performance is the gateway to personal success. The concept of team performance is introduced to them, yet somehow it is not perceived as equal to the individual effort. Clyde Drexler, Michael Jordan, Larry Bird, Magic Johnson, Karl Malone, David Robinson, Wayne Gretzky, Michael Milken, Jim Robinson, Lee Iacocca, and the stars of any profession are all examples of people who receive more praise for their individual efforts than do the teams for which they play. Every organization has key players whose job performance is valued more than that of others. Thus, while organizations preach team performance, they value the act of the individual. The message given to employees is "do as I say, not as I do." Cognitive dissonance becomes the norm of the organization where employees sense a level of dishonesty in the stated organizational ethos portrayed to the world. The question for organizations, then, is deciding what level of individualism is valued versus what level of team performance is needed. It is hard for employees to listen to the team-effort statements of the managers when management behavior suggests that personal effort exceeds group effort. Granted, groupthink is not perceived positively; however, group action seems to be valued. When the individual is rewarded for individual effort, questions arise.

In the struggle between individual and group effort, trauma becomes a way of life for employees. Think back to your rise within an organization. How often did you wonder if your individual effort was sufficient to allow you to advance up the organizational ladder? How many successes did you have to generate to be noticed by the organizational leadership? How often did you hear management express the necessity for increased team performance, yet how often did you rely on one employee to carry a project? The process of cognitive dissonance—that is, balancing individuality with the need for team performance—is a traumatic process for the person and the organization. When the trauma continues and when little work toward improvement occurs, escalation of violent perceptions occurs, and the cycle of violence continues.

Embracing versus Discounting Ideas and Ideals

Usually, persons become uncomfortable or traumatized by the process of discounting. When this process becomes a pattern of behavior, the discounted person often becomes violent or angry. Thus, the process of discounting is a violent act.

"Sarah" works for a major utility corporation. She received her degree in computer science with a specialization in geographic mapping. For three years, she has worked for a superior who cuts her off in meetings, downplays the importance of her work, makes sexist jokes, and generally disregards Sarah's potential. Sarah reports numerous reasons for her anger. She states that her boss is rude, sexist, and disrespectful. However, she feels that the largest indignity and the most insidious behavior of her boss is his continual discount of her ideas and her potential to help the organization. Sarah's feelings are often shared by employees in government, private industry, academia, and nonprofit associations.

The nature of the discount is to disregard or throw away the views or perspective of others. It implies a baseline of homogeneity existing within another person or organization. Diversity is perceived as a non-value, while homogeneity is the norm for acceptance and inclusion among peers and superiors. Young managers may experience discount from their elders within an organization. Women may experience the discount from male counterparts. Minorities may experience the discounts from the majority. The cycle of violence grows as discounts become the norm.

A. J. Muste, author of "The Situation and Program of Christianity" (*Religion in Life* 8 [1939], pp. 223–224), states that systems are comprised of human beings living in particular relationships. The only occurrences within a system are interactions among human beings. Discounting in a system results in a lack of interactions, thus nothing happens within that system. Muste's meaning is that organizations can "include" minorities, women, and elderly persons within the organization without involving them in the real life of the organization. In this case, no inclusiveness occurs, so the only outcome is the discount of these groups.

Discounts have traditionally created conflicts among members of organizations. Where the discounts have been institutionalized, oppressive environments develop, creating violent reactions from those feeling oppressed. Labor unions are typical examples of groups of systemically discounted people that have been formed to create a sense of legitimacy and equity. The American Civil Liberties Union, Gay activists, African-

American activists, and other ethnic groups are examples of discounted, frustrated persons or groups determined to create equity and legitimacy.

Discounts, therefore, are catalysts for violent perceptions and actions. Unfortunately, society in general and organizations in particular grapple for strategies to implement change incrementally, thereby continuing to fuel the fires of change. Organizations often get the message but look at legitimacy without equity. Then oppressed, discounted persons shift their focus from equity to liberation and work toward total systems change, when a "tweak" of the system would have been more appropriate. Hence, the violent cycle continues.

Control, Power, and Authority Issues

Employees often describe their organizations as vassals of control, power, and authority, the purveyors of Machiavellian logic. I believe that these titles are too harsh; however, there is a grain of truth to them. During the 1980s, organizations appeared to focus more on the individualistic goal of management/organizational rights—unions and employees be damned! The underlying issue during this period was the organization's desire to take up arms against issues of runaway costs, ineffective managerial performance, poor training for employees, and deficiency in work performance. Methodologies involved curbing the influence and authority of unions, shifting accountability for productivity to managers, and rewriting the guiding principles of the organizations in policy documents and procedural manuals. The process was two tiered—specifically, incremental change in shifting the organizational ethos for the employees, and dramatic change in policy direction for organizations. The process focused on the issues of power, authority, and control.

In my book *The Congruence of People and Organizations: Healing Dysfunction from the Inside Out* (Westport, CT: Quorum Books, 1993), I speak of organizations operating from underlying belief structures that dictate certain styles of policy directions. Power, authority, and control become both outcomes and methodologies in organizational life. Where it is clear that power, authority, and control are organizational outcomes, fewer perceptions of organizational violence occur. Where power, authority, and control are methodologies for initiating action or expunging diversity and difference, organizational violence is rampant in the perspectives of employees and managers.

Power, authority, and control are tenets of violence when the desired outcome is to defeat an opponent, superior, or subordinate. The lines of interaction are drawn to compete in unhealthy strategies rather than to collaborate to win on an issue. Burrough's book *Vendetta* describes American Express as an organization poised to defeat and destroy Safra, president of the Swiss division of American Express, with power, authority, and control. In the end, the consumption of corporate officers with defeating another caused them to lose sight of the issue of fair competition. Other examples of violent organizational control are the sabotage of management information systems as suggested in H. Ross Perot's desire to stop General Motors, and Howard Hughes's desire to maintain power in the defense industry by fabricating test results on his company's airplane parts. Each approach was designed to defeat or control opponents, not to compete fairly. Each approach was designed to generate fear in the opponent. Because of such attempts to defeat, generate fear, and expunge diversity and difference, the process of violence continues.

Means versus the Ends: A Process of Dichotomy

Probably the largest dynamic in the issue of organizational violence is the dichotomy of ends justifying the means versus the means becoming the end. This issue is one of ethical management and performance within organizational life. The following questions arise: Is it the role of organizations to create strategies that work to defeat others in order for the world view of the organization to win? Or is it more important for organizations to create strategies that allow the values and ethics of the organization to shine through in its actions and decisions? It appears that these ethical question is not asked often enough in the board rooms and managerial meetings of organizations today.

Trauma and violence are outgrowths of rationalizations made to justify pain that has been created when an individual or organization is attacked versus an issue or problem being resolved. Too often, strategies focus on the individual or organization, not on the issue or problem that impedes growth, profitability, or performance.

THE TRADITIONAL VESSELS OF VIOLENCE

In the previous section, the tenets of violence are described as the absence of key components in the developmental process of people and organizational systems. This section addresses those traditional and well-known instruments—vessels, if you will—that implement violent strategies. You might ask why they are called *traditional*, or *technical*, vessels of violence. They are traditional because they are time-tested, and they are technical because of the nature of the processes. These vessels or approaches are:

1. policies
2. procedures

3. administrative regulations

4. labor agreements

5. hiring practices

6. organizational structures

7. supervisory development and implementation

Management and employees have become literal in their responses or reactions to situations that impact organizational performance. The standard for change has become a process of focusing on symptoms as the issues of dysfunction within organizational life. These symptoms are far from the real issues in assessing violence. Current organizational approaches designed to eradicate violence focus on time management, total quality management to alter existing practices, team building, structural changes, strategic planning from a structure and program direction, confrontation avoidance and conflict resolution, human resource training, technical training, and affirmative action programs. Each process becomes an ill-fated attempt at real change because it is not substantive in nature. However, it is important to identify and recognize the traditional vessels of violence in order to effectively move beyond them to substantive vessels.

Policies

Policies are principles that guide a course of action within organizational life. Policies are the boundary setters of organizational behavior and describe the parameters under which individuals make or create decisions for congruence between organizational direction and organizational and personal action. Unfortunately, policies often avoid ensuring that their purpose is clearly understood. Take the aforementioned *L.A. Times* articles for example. Where were the policies that would have helped in balancing the reported actions of some executives? What were the checks that existed that would have inhibited managers of the mentioned organizations from believing that their organizations would tolerate this form of behavior? Some will say that the checks and balances were present. Others will say that the policies were too broad and left too much room for interpretation. Still others will say that the policies were designed broadly to allow this degree of unethical behavior on the part of management. Regardless of which perspective is taken, the reality suggests that the policies did not do their job, and, thus, violence to the organization, its employees, and its clients was the outcome. If a policy is inappropriate, ineffectual, or just plain bad, the outcome is sure to be the same.

Procedures

Procedure is the act, method or manner—the sequence of steps to be followed in the implementation of a given goal that actualizes a policy. Where policies are bad or inappropriate, procedures are inappropriate. However, procedures are often developed to circumvent bad policy. Unfortunately, two things occur in this case: the policy itself, although determined to be ineffective, is not rewritten to make it effective (*perspective*), and the one developing such procedure determines what is best for the organization and the employee (*value set*). In effect, the organization now has myriad policy makers and procedure setters with different perspectives and different value sets.

As multiple webs are developed and as numerous values drive the procedures, confusion, frustration, trauma, and dysfunction affect the employee and the organization. Violent reactions by employees arise as attempts to find a true path for appropriate behavior within the organization. Theologian James Cone, in his book *Liberation* said, "Is there knowledge of God independent of the Bible? The question is irrelevant. It is not the theologian's task to settle logical problems unrelated to the affairs of men. It is his task to speak to his times, pointing to God's revelation in the events around him" (Philadelphia: J. P. Lippincott Company, 1970, p. 98). A transposition of the concept would be: Is there knowledge of the desires of the organization without effective policy? It is not the executive's, manager's, or employee's task to define policy for the organization to guide performance. Rather, it is the task of the executive, manager, or employee to implement actions pointing to the policy as the guiding revelation of the events planned and implemented around him or her.

Administrative Regulations

Administrative regulations are specific governing rules for managing the work to be performed within the organization. The regulations also define the organization's perspective on employment, retirement, benefits, and ethics. The regulations are an outgrowth of the guiding principles of organizational policy. Where an organization speaks to empowerment of employees within its policy, regulations should embrace this concept. Where the policy expressly speaks to equitable and fair treatment of employees, then supervision, work assignment, and bargaining agreements should embrace these concepts of equity and fairness. Where the policy speaks to team performance, customer service, and quality, the regulations should spell out guidelines for these. In effect, the regulations are the rules that define behavior and attitude within the organization. Where policies are clear but regulations contradict the policy; where policies are unclear and regulations are restrictive and fear oriented; where regulations focus on control and authority, dehumanizing the potential of the employee to embrace the organization; or where executive management implements regulations and does not check to assess the congruence of organization behavior to the regulations, violence occurs.

Labor Agreements

The process of bargaining is a truly conflictual and competitive experience in American business and government. Each side professes to want an amiable and equitable experience for the good of the whole; yet each appears to work toward defeat of the other. I recently worked with a bargaining unit and a governmental agency to look at the process of collaboration for a win-win negotiated settlement. Although a positive outcome was derived for agreement by the two parties, I was struck by the amount of time required to implement trust through a bonding process, inclusion through a unique labor/management strategic development process, and building congruence rather than dichotomy through an ethics marriage within the organization. I was struck by the almost paranoid existence that management and labor had created. Clinically, the behaviors of both management and labor reflected a borderline personality disorder; theologically, the behavior mirrored Gabriel Vahanian's Death of God theology; and socially, the behaviors represented the adjustment-failure concepts of psychodynamic and social theorists.

The violence inherent in labor agreements is the belief that neither side can be trusted. The *letter* of the law is the binding glue, yet no *spirit* of the law appears to permeate the behaviors of organizations and unions. Both the organization and the union members are the losers. The stance in confrontation management and the policy is win what you can. Policies, procedures, and administrative regulations are disregarded; defeating the other is the only goal.

Hiring Practices

I recently spoke to a group of minority consultants whose expertise was in human resource management and development. In asking them the most troubling issue they experienced in trying to be ethical with their clients, they responded that helping the organization to address its hiring practice was the most difficult. The consultants felt that management and the organizations delude themselves into believing that "the best fit" becomes a legitimate criterion for selection. They spoke of trying to help managers balance their "best fit" with organizational policy that speaks of diversity in the work force, equal opportunity, and

affirmative action goals. They talked about the disconnectedness of training programs on diversity with the lack of a diverse work force, and
they marveled at the blinders placed on organizations concerning their
behavior.

Organizations create violence in their hiring practices by not ensuring
that fairness and equity are the underlying parameters for hiring new
employees. Personnel managers report that they are meeting the needs
of management and are including management in the selection process.
When asked about the adherence to organizational policy, cultural
norms, and values, they report that their actions have been equitable.
However, saying that one is an "equal opportunity employer" is not
enough to create a belief that fairness and equity exist. Personnel departments become vessels of violence in their acquiescence to management values, rather than leaders of organizational policy describing the
organizational ethos and culture. Too often, organizations embrace difference and newness as long as it is not a threat or does not alter the
status quo. When challenged, organizations resort to varying interpretations of the rules or the law. There is a convenient forgetfulness regarding the policies that are to *guide* organizational action.

Organizational Structures

The Arizona Nuclear Power Project was a subsidiary organization of
the Arizona Public Service Corporation. Both organizations maintained
highly tiered organizational structures to ensure that regulatory compliance to all utility and nuclear environments was not violated. In 1985,
a problem existed because the nuclear regulatory environment required
quick decision making that was not conducive to a tiered organizational
structure. Managements of the two corporations went round and round
regarding effective decision making to reduce the costs that could occur
from imprudent decision making. The organization ultimately determined that two structures could exist: tiered relationships at top management levels for consistency and congruence with organizational
imperatives, and a flatter and more horizontal structure for the actual
management of the nuclear facility. This worked well for the organization and its management. However, getting to the change created
numerous problems that survived long after the change itself. Employees
felt that their expertise in varying aspects of nuclear development and
management was discounted. Managers felt torn between doing the
right thing and choosing the politically astute option. Fear of termination
in a right-to-work environment caused more protective stances by employees, and managers thereby made a large number of imprudent decisions within the organization. The structure created a sense of trauma

that spilled over to violent and restrictive behaviors by employees of the organization.

In many organizations, structure is an impediment to success. Structure is a cause of pain and trauma and blocks growth and development. In some organizations it impedes profitability and is diametrically opposite of policies that are meant to guide organizational and personal performance.

Supervisory Development and Implementation

In every organization for which I consult, employees and managers complain about the "band-aid management process." The band-aid management process supports the concept of doing enough to "stay" the problem and providing just enough training to employees to get over the hump. Band-aid work is a very violent experience within organizations. Band-aid work says that I know what the problem is, I know how to fix it, however, the band-aid will suffice. In this scenario, effectiveness is not important; maintaining organizational life as it has always been is the underlying goal. Policies and procedures are tossed aside, as are the needs and wishes of the employees; the belief is that there are always others who are willing to do the work.

The violent process discounts the necessity to mold and develop employees and systems into an efficient, hardworking machine to achieve realistic and achievable outcomes for the organization and the employees. Employees and organizational systems often need prodding to respond to rather than react against needed alterations of existing thoughts and actions. What would be helpful in expunging violence would be revisiting the policies that guide the choices made by organizations and its leadership. It makes sense to shift and stop this restrictive and protective process that has been created. However, how do we stop?

THE VOLATILE ORGANIZATION, THE VOLATILE PERSON

I think the critical dynamic in looking at organizational violence is recognizing that too much time has been spent trying to compartmentalize the issues of organizational life. Theorists often talk about the issues of management or the issues of labor, such as control of either. Theorists address strategies for impacting policies or procedures. Consultants intervene in organizational life sometimes codependently to fix this or that, to resolve a conflict or intervene to become a partner in some fashion of incremental change. Yet, organizational violence continues because the real issue of the relationship between the organization and the individual is substantively overlooked. Denial of that key factor sets in motion the issues of violence, and volatility becomes the lifelong strategy that is incrementally addressed by both the organization and the person.

Organizations benefit from employees, and employees conversely benefit from the organization. This is not to say that the benefits are equal but that the benefits, both positive and negative, exist. Of concern are the issue of influence, the issue of give and take, the issue of creation versus maintenance, the issue of maintenance versus entrepreneurship, and the issue of what works versus what is taught out of frustration with lack of congruity around what will work to create and sustain organizations and people. Discounting the relationship allows us all to lose and continue to perpetuate our own violent experiences. We, people and organizations, are constantly relating to one another as though there were no relationship between us. We are constantly experiencing mutual influence with one another. If we are to change, we must recognize that influence is created and accepted because of one's understanding of the varying facets of one's roles within the organization, as an individual, and in the society or community at large. We must recognize that our vested interests are tied to one another, and only through recognizing and responding to those interests on multiple levels can we jointly build credibility, security, and accomplishments toward any number of outcomes.

Influence, direction, acceptance of roles, responsibilities, accountability, inclusiveness, balancing of individual and team, time, responsiveness, and ethical choices—all these are essential in the creation of effective bonds. When we experience the void created by the absence of any of the aforementioned, we experience a volatile reaction. Lack of courage to challenge and explore our choices and decisions also creates volatility.

The following chapters address approaches to understanding the dynamics of violence and how we do not just stop the cycle but alter the cycle to a more effective and productive process of change. It is not important to tell specifically how to alter the policies and procedures but how to prescriptively develop strategies for expunging violence and creating just means and ends to products, services, and management and policy development. We start that process in chapter two with a look at the substance of violence and its impact on organization performance.

2

The Substance of Violence: How We Block Our Integrity

John is a professor of business management at a major university in Atlanta, Georgia. He experiences major frustration in trying to convey to students the problem with management, and ultimately the problem with education: the theories are outdated and ineffective. Even with this belief and knowledge, John continues to teach theories and strategies that are ineffective.

George is the entrepreneur of an organization that has been in existence for seven years. He got his business up and running because of a deep commitment to the concept of service delivery to his potential customers. The experts, consultants, and management gurus told George that his organizational success would be enhanced and maintained by hiring key professionals with management and administrative backgrounds. George thought the advice was sound and hired the management suggested. Seven years later, he is mired in union battles, management layers ineffective in moving his commitment to continual action, and employees disgruntled with the state of the company.

Joyce is the training and development manager for a major municipal government. Within executive staff meetings, she speaks of the problems expressed by employees concerning accomplishing their work, feeling included in the decisions, and relating to management. Management states that maintaining the organization is the highest need at the moment and that the traditional training programs that have been used within the organization should be continued. Joyce complies with the direction.

Each of these situations are examples of organizational violence at its insidious and substantive core.

Organizational violence substantively encompasses greed, envy, gluttony, pride, maintenance, and fear. These key dynamics define the parameters that create and perpetuate violence in organizational and personal development. Organizations—public, private, and nonprofit—continually fall prey to the maintenance dynamics of organizational systems and the fear dynamics of individuals managing and guiding the direction of the organization. If one feels oppressed by the actions of the organization, the unfortunate approach is to develop strategies that focus on the creation of strength as a reaction to potential exploitation. If one feels in charge of the actions of the organization, the approach is to maintain the status quo. Neither approach acknowledges or embraces the concepts of creation on the part of individuals participating in the organization or entrepreneurship in the design and strategy of organization development.

The entrenchment of violence is, therefore, substantiated by embracing three theoretical stances that define organizations' and people's reactions to change, newness, and diversity. These three stances are balance of power, freedom of association, and incongruous competition.

BALANCE OF POWER

Organizations and people begin to focus on "balance of power" strategies when fear becomes the behavioral direction for organizational and personal decision making. This strategy focuses on organizational power as a check and balance against other power groups, such as unions, competitive corporations, and other trade association posturing. If management is strong, labor unions should become strong. If the military complex is too strong, then the civilian complex should become equally strong. The theory suggests that the use of "power checks" becomes a process of creating equity and equilibrium among the competing groups, thereby expunging powerlessness from the masses.

There is a problem with the balance-of-power theory as described above. When power is used to contain and establish boundaries for groups and ideas, power itself becomes a controlling process designed to make the status quo tolerable for all who experience it in organizational and personal life. The premise becomes an approach to suggest to people and systems that "balance" is created by posturing toward winning. A good example of this balance-of-power theory was the growth of the defense industry during the Reagan-Bush years. Presidents Ronald Reagan and George Bush believed that the creation of power checks would create equity. Unfortunately, fear was the outcome of the balance of power approach because the other components of a healthy organizational system were not balanced. Reagan and Bush forgot to bond with the country on the critical elements of balance: education, collaboration, diversity, trust, and congruence. Instead, they focused on the critical elements of imbalance: fear, maintenance, greed, gluttony, competition, and homogeneity.

Each of the elements of imbalance is designed to separate and distance one person or group from another. When you instill fear; you force your opponent to relinquish personal power to you in order to increase your stature. When you focus on maintenance of the status quo and have the authority to ensure that maintenance is the desired outcome in your approaches to business decisions, you defeat the creativity of the persons you employ and the products or service you generate. When greed, and gluttony are your desired outcomes, decisions are focused toward the short term, and actions are self-directed rather than group or organizational directed. When management and organizational leaders use any of these perspectives in defining the direction of the organization, ethics becomes a major ballast driving in the sea, and organizations and their employees ultimately suffer.

FREEDOM OF ASSOCIATION

The second violence theory is the concept of freedom of association. This theoretical perspective represents like-minded corporations or individuals banding together to create options and strategies that advance their special view. Health care industry groups, the tobacco industry, auto industry groups, social libertarians, educators, and numerous other groups expend energy and resources to convince others that their perspective is the best for the country.

Members of organizations employing freedom of association experience frustration in that decisions are made for them and without their input, creating a feeling of powerlessness. There is little attempt to consider the responsibility of the organization to advance good public policy, only organizational or group policy. Rationalization of this strategy is based on the capital idea that resources are expended based on a group response to perceived issues—that is, groupthink—for a perspective that controls the behavior and choices of others. Control is maintained by the reduction of diverse perspectives and collaborative ventures.

In his book *Victims of Groupthink* (Boston: Houghton Mifflin, 1972), Irving Janis says that the utilization of groupthink creates an illusion of invulnerability, which leads to a mistaken belief that "we cannot lose." He states, "the more amiability and esprit de corps among the members of a policy-making 'in-group,' the greater the danger that independent, critical thinking will be replaced by 'groupthink,' which is likely to result in irrational and dehumanizing actions directed against 'out-groups.' "

INCONGRUOUS COMPETITION

In American society, competition has been seen as an effective approach for developing new ideas for research and the creation of new products. The concept of competition is supported by sports, test scores, dating, religious beliefs, and homogeneous practices. There is a level of incongruence in the competitive strategies existing within organizational and personal life. The incongruence is the inability to effectively find a balance between building people and building systems toward an outcome that fosters creativity. Instead, the concept of competition pits one against another, with the outcome of defeat of the other as the primary goal.

In my first book, *The Congruence of People and Organizations: Healing Dysfunction from the Inside Out* (Westport, CT: Quorum Books, 1993), I tried to describe the incongruity of people's actions with their underlying belief systems. In this book, I am stating that the process of being incongruous perpetuates violence in organizational life. The desired outcomes we envision contribute substantially to the violence that occurs. We create dichotomies in our behavior based on a strategy of competition. Discussions in organizations talk of teams, yet individual performance is more valued. We suggest becoming collaborative in our approach to developing work products, yet we create competitive strategies for beating our business competitors to the delivery of a product. We speak of integrity, yet we commit organizational sabotage as an attempt to get ahead. In each of these approaches, and in much of organizational life, we function in a dichotomous fashion that is incongruent with our statements of mission, supervision of staff, and development of people. We seem to believe that employees and our clients do not recognize that something is wrong.

Each of these approaches resorts to violence because of our incapacity to confront and create strategies for fundamental questions in our lives. Each of these approaches limits our vision and forces people to fit into a mold to create comfort rather than addressing the critical issues of organizational business, organizational change, organizational growth and innovation, resource development and allocation, ineffective cost structuring, and quality of product, services, and staff.

Look at the words used in the previous paragraphs: power checks, equity, checks and balances, strength, competition, powerlessness. The words alone speak to winners and losers, gain and loss, control and being controlled, oppression and exploitation, maintenance and fear. They describe the process of management and labor, but also the process of violence. If you subscribe to the balance of power model, the freedom of association model, or the incongruous competition model, then you assume that groupthink, group control, and outcome manipulation achieve sufficient power and strength to keep in check the power and strength of other groups, thereby achieving a certain degree of freedom from the control of others and equity within the system.

We often agree with only one portion of the perspective of any group to which we belong. We may avoid sharing our own perspectives for fear of the consequences from others. As a result, we may participate in activities and behaviors that reduce self-respect. There are times when pride guides our decision making, when greed and envy are guideposts for our choices, and when maintenance and fear dictate our responses to perceived wrongs within an organization. For example, we may participate in or benefit from the abuse of another. We then rationalize these outcomes as just the results of competition, power checks, and freedom of association. We may privately regret not acting, not challenging, not being ourselves for the sake of the job, the promotion, the raise. We perpetuate violence by our silence or our cunning.

THE INTEGRITY DILEMMA

Integrity is an issue of ethics in organizational life. Ethics provides the precondition for the creation of effective organizational and public policy. It is the precursor to any single policy or action within organizations. Chapter one discusses a number of articles that address the issue of integrity and ethics on the part of leaders of organizations. In each case, ethical misconduct or the lack of integrity is the issue that overshadows the actions of the organization. Appearance is the critical issue. In actuality, appearing to do the wrong thing while doing the right thing is still doing the wrong thing. There is a moral dimension given to the issue of public ethics. Every corporation is held accountable for the actions of its officers and for the underlying belief of fair play.

Take, for example, a gender discrimination suit filed by female employees within a private, garment corporation. These employees report that management unfairly compensates them for their services while giving higher salaries to males in comparable work assignments. The case is investigated, and the legal perspective says that management is within its right to compensate differently; however, management recognizes that today, the appearance of being wrong can create more harm than actually being right. Management determines that equal compensation is more cost effective than the loss of women as customers because of a *perceived* injustice—an appearance standard.

There are also organizational standards that guide ethical performance and integrity. Every major trade association, such as the American Medical Association, the American Bankers Association, the Securities and Exchange Commission, the American Psychological Association, the American Civil Liberties Union, and numerous others, believes that both the appearance standard and an organizational standard are required to effectively help employees recognize the boundaries that impact their scope of authority and creativity within an organization. This boundary is an organization's method for establishing group ethics and group integrity to ensure that the customer-client base is not eroded by poor decision making. One method is equal to the other for the organization, while appearance is more critical for the public and the customer-client base.

The American Society for Public Administration's (ASPA) Code of Ethics describes a governmental prescribed plan for ethical performance, as depicted in Table 2.1. This ethical code demonstrates the efforts of an organization to effectively manage the process of ethics and integrity. However, we sometimes fail to recognize that legislating ethical performance does not mean that organizational traumas will not occur. Everyone does not recognize that his or her ethical performance is out of synch with the organization regardless of the directions given. To that extent, it becomes important to assess the ethical breeds that seem to guide the actions of people and organizations.

ETHICAL BREEDS

Ethics strategies within organizations seem to flow in a continuum from the craftiest to the most open and direct. These strategies are embodied in various ethical "breeds," represented by animals of the jungle. Organizational life mirrors that of the jungle. When the law of the jungle is respected, life there continues to prosper and bear reasonable fruit for sustenance and growth. When that law is disrespected, ravaged, and disregarded as an essential component of continued life, then the jungle becomes harsh, lashing back with floods, erosion of the land, the absence of life-sustaining vegetation, and the decline of growth. Likewise, when the organization and its management adhere to ethical principles, valuing the clients and customers and the employees, the organization is successful in the marketplace. When the organization creates a violent organizational history, violating the employees and the public trust of the client base, then the balance of power strategies occur within the organization that work toward its defeat.

The ethical breeds on the continuum are the *cobra, the chameleon, the ostrich, the antelope, the lion,* and *the eagle.* Each animal represents behaviors consistent with varying strategies of ethical behavior and management. Each animal is capable of greed, gluttony, fear, and lust, as are organizations. They display behaviors that can mirror the attributes

Table 2.1
American Society for Public Administration's Code of Ethics

- Demonstrate the highest standards of personal integrity, truthfulness, honesty and fortitude in all our public institutions.

- Serve in such a way that we do not realize undue personal gain from the performance of our official duties.

- Avoid any interest or activity which is in conflict with the conduct of our official duties.

- Support, implement, and promote merit employment and programs of affirmative action to assure equal employment opportunity by our recruitment, selection, and advancement of qualified persons from all elements of society.

- Eliminate all forms of illegal discrimination, fraud, and mismanagement of public funds, and support colleagues if they are in difficulty because of responsible efforts to correct such discrimination, fraud, mismanagement or abuse.

- Serve the public with respect, concern, courtesy and responsiveness, recognizing that service to the public is beyond service to oneself.

- Strive for personal professional excellence and encourage the professional development of our associates and those seeking to enter the field of public administration.

- Approach our organization and operational duties with a positive attitude and constructively support open communication, creativity, dedication and compassion.

- Respect and protect the privileged information to which we have access in the course of our official duties.

- Exercise whatever discretionary authority we have under law to promote the public interest.

- Accept as a personal duty the responsibility to keep up to date on emerging issues and to administer the public business with professional competence, fairness, impartiality, efficiency and effectiveness.

- Respect, support, study, and when necessary, work to improve federal and state constitutions and other laws which define the relationships among public agencies, employees, clients, and all citizens.

ASPA's Code of Ethics Guidelines adopted by ASPA, March 27, 1985.

of pride, competition, and trust. Each one's approach to relating to its environment is based on characteristics of history, tradition, challenges, and power; and each animal succeeds when it respects the environment and its fellow beasts of the jungle. Organizations often operate through competitive strategies, historical approaches, traditional perspectives, and power options; and organizations that can effectively respond to the alterations of their environments, their markets, and their products/ services thrive in the open marketplace. Organizations are comprised of all these breeds, and organizations succeed or fail based on their ability to balance the different beasts.

The Cobra

The cobra is considered to be one of the deadliest reptiles on the planet. The snake creates a fascination because of its hood and coloring. The snake is known for mesmerizing its victims prior to striking a deadly blow. It strategically stalks its prey and chooses those creatures that are vulnerable to attack based on deficiencies in their mettle. Additionally, they are known to devour their spouses. Numerous movies have been made about the cobra, with varying degrees of accuracy regarding the snake's characteristics. In some movies, the cobra is shown getting longer by devouring other species of snakes because they are less strong, virile, and crafty. In other movies, it is shown as a possessive creature that destroys a man's loves in order to possess the man. In still other movies, the cobra is shown as the idol of scientists trying to recreate the snake as the supreme being, the envy of all mankind. Emotional characteristics assigned to the snake include the personification of evil, the master of vicious stealth, and the creature never to be trusted.

The organizational cobra has very much the same characteristics. The organizational cobra plots and schemes to take advantage of situations that increase the market share and is usually sinister, creating fear in colleagues and competitors. The organizational cobra is a possessive creature, determined to ensure that defeat of the opposing person, system, or group is attained. Usually, the organizational cobra is a gifted, eloquent professional that makes positive headway within the organization. Assignments are taken readily with great success. Promotions are forthcoming with larger, broader, sweeping assignments. The cobra component begins to raise its head when assignments begin to define or directly reflect the direction of organizational policy. The adherence to a code of ethics seems far fetched; rather, performance is defined by the overall objective. The objective is beyond winning; the objective is defeat of another. Thus, the cobra has a character flaw or personality flaw—a lack of conscience or societal judgment. In Bryan Burrough's book *Vendetta: American Express and the Smearing of Edmond Safra* (New York: HarperCollins, 1992), numerous characters represent the cobra. Burrough speaks of an unscrupulous reporter/writer named Greco.

> In mid-December, Greco did a curious thing; he faxed Roberto [Jim Robinson] a copy of an American news wire story on the Republic of Miami [a bank] indictment. Greco's faxing of the story to Roberto

raises questions about the lengths to which he was willing to go to smear Safra. Was Greco simply mixed up? Did he not realize the two banks were unconnected? Or had he grown so intent on smearing Safra he was willing to intentionally mislead a reporter as to which Republic Bank had been indicted? (p. 399)

In organizations, the political desire to be in charge is often a mirror of Greco's behavior. Directors, managers, supervisors, and leaders all exhibit the behavior of cobras, justifying their actions for the good of the company.

The Chameleon

The chameleon is a lizard that can change its coloring to correspond to its environment. It uses its gifts of camouflage either to avoid trouble or to attack its prey. The chameleon can devour with a flash of the tongue. Remaining hidden, its existence is forgotten, causing one to focus elsewhere while it continues its predatory nature.

The military values this creature highly. Tactics include camouflaging oneself with makeup, clothing, and branches and leaves as well as using camouflaged vehicles. The art of disguise is the chameleon's forte. In the espionage or undercover arena, disguise becomes a means of gaining trust from the persons to be deceived or destroyed.

In the world of sports, the chameleon is the forgotten player on the field or court—the one who comes through with the outside shot, the tight end forgotten by the defense. In fact, this creature is revered in the art of competition, including organizational competition.

The organizational chameleon is the professional violator. This is the individual who seemingly becomes your ally, learns your secrets, and emotionally violates you behind your back. The chameleon survives because we marvel at the cleverness displayed in his or her actions. We are surprised by the disguise, awed at the survivability, fooled by the tactics, and reproached for doubting the sincerity of the chameleon. We aid in our own demise when we trust and believe the chameleon. The chameleon represents the successful competitor, the survivor in the individualistic quest to reach the top of the organizational ladder.

In the governmental organization, the chameleon is the consummate politician—one who can change his or her perspective with the changes in the wind. The 1992 election season appeared to be a referendum on the chameleon. There was a movement to peel off the stripes of the chameleon and discover the true colors and substance of the politician. The lifelong bureaucrat is also a chameleon. The bureaucrat changes with each administration, recognizing what "colors" are required to stay on top or to survive the onslaught of change. The bureaucrat is the ultimate chameleon because survival within the organization is the highest need. The bureaucrat, like the chameleon, changes colors—positioned to ensure survival even when commitment is lacking for the changed position. Stories are constantly told of the injustice of the politician. Marcos, Duvalier, and Amin were all chameleons. Ronald Reagan was dubbed the "Teflon President," but the "Chameleon President" might have been a more appropriate label for he survived politically despite his immoral disregard for the majority while valuing the beliefs of a few.

The Ostrich

The ostrich is a unique creature. It is graceful in its walk and swift on its feet. However, the ostrich is a dumb creature. It believes that hiding its head in the sand will keep it from harm. The ostrich believes that seeing no evil means that none exists. It is not a bad or deceitful creature, but is often blindly and unknowingly violated and destroyed because of sticking its head in the sand.

The organizational ostrich is characteristic of the majority of the members of an organization. Too often, employees, managers, and executives blindly stick their heads in the sand, causing themselves to be violated by choosing not to actively participate in their survival or development. The ostrich will know that something is wrong but choose not to look, not to question, or not to speak out against an assignment or directive that does not make sense. He or she will look the other way while a coworker is castigated unfairly. The ostrich will watch the destruction of another, knowing it is wrong, and saying "it will just go away."

We are struggling organizationally in the United States because we have for too long functioned as the cobra, the chameleon, and the ostrich. We have little commitment to ideals, principles, or practices because we have found avenues to justify our violations of others and of ourselves; and we have found ways of blaming another. President Bush blamed Congress for not implementing a domestic policy. Recalling his words, "I will do anything to win this election," one might ask, "Is this man capable of embodying an ideal or principle, or is he an example of a cobra, chameleon, or ostrich?"

Being an ethical breed is not always a negative experience. There is a lot we can learn from other creatures, as well. As stated earlier, the concept of ethical "beasts" provides an opportunity for us to explore positive avenues for accepting change, coexisting with others, and adhering to ideals, principles, and practices.

The Antelope

The antelope is a more positive creature. It is graceful, light on its feet, surefooted in the mountains or on rough terrain, and gentle to its surroundings. It coexists with the other animals in its environment. It does not take advantage of others, yet it seems to grow in a healthy and respected manner. The antelope is a team player, often traveling in a herd and being concerned for the well-being of the herd.

Unfortunately, the antelope is often too predictable, being destroyed by predators. Hunters also desire the antlers of the antelope. Besting the antelope at its gracefulness is laudable.

Within organizations, the antelope is the consummate team player. The organizational antelope is the person with multiple approaches to an idea or ideal. The predictable behavior of the antelope causes peers, subordinates, and superiors to trust the organizational antelope and believe that coexistence is a valuable trait of this beast. The organizational antelope looks at work groups, intact in structure, as the focus for effectiveness and change. He or she is not focused on power and control but rather on the creation of a better team to blend into the organization. The critical attribute is the absence of volatility on the part of the beast; however, there is concern that the organizational antelope does not sufficiently challenge or question the behaviors and choices of the leader.

A co-worker at a large county governmental agency was the consummate team player, believing that his focus on the team would provide the perfect blend for the organization. He would acquiesce and change his views if he believed that the change would cause a consensus agreement or avoid a conflict. Unfortunately, his perspective on organizational process often caused him not to provide his expertise in discussions surrounding work products or change. He believed that management wanted a team-oriented approach, not his individual view, to work productivity. When management was forced to reduce personnel based on economic considerations, he was layed off as a part of the effort. His superiors explained that the reason for this was that his total focus on the team made him too gullible and ineffective. They needed a better balance between individualism and teamwork. He was shattered, but like the antelope, took the high ground to enhance his skills and gracefully move forward in his professional career. He was a winner, for he stood fast to his principles that did not violate others.

The Lion

The lion is known as the "king of the jungle." The lion is graceful but strong. The lion is aggressive when survival is the needed outcome. It is protective of its young, yet allows them freedom to develop critical skills. The lion is respectful of the other creatures of the jungle, recognizing whether or not to challenge a larger beast. Its individual abilities display themselves in combat, hunting, and exploration. Lions utilize these same traits in a team effort when achieving the outcome requires more than one animal. The lion is direct in approach, clear about its place in the hierarchy of the jungle, and respectful of those incidents where defeat is the inevitable outcome.

The organizational lion is both respected and, unfortunately, feared within the organization. Where organizations use hierarchy and authority to dictate process and action, the lion seems to take all the credit for the outcome. The organizational lion is usually straightforward and does not "play games," therefore generating admiration and respect for adherence to a specific approach. However, because he or she is apart and different, other organization members fear that he or she cannot be controlled. The organizational lion embodies a process of courage and ethics, struggling to maintain a belief in his or her skills regardless of the behaviors of the organization. The organizational lion risks being himself or herself—focused, clear, direct, and effective.

The Eagle

The eagle is free to soar on the winds of change and the fierce currents of disharmony. The eagle thrives on its ability to be in control of itself and its ability to meld effectively with its environment. Able to survey the entire landscape, the eagle is in the best position to make choices about its surroundings, food, and balance. The eagle is a creature of commitment; historically, they are monogamous, building relationships that last. The eagle is known as an excellent provider and parent to its young. It is strong, self-assured, graceful, simplicity in motion.

The organizational eagle reflects this simplicity as well. Not concerned with politics or crafty strategies, the organizational eagle focuses on understanding the organizational system in action. Rather than struggling amidst the entanglement of the organizational "forest," the organizational eagle surveys the forest from above and creates strategies that aim toward accomplishing organizational goals. The eagle becomes the organization's most focused, ethical person. Dedicated to excellence, he or she focuses on the reduction of barriers, the elimination of waste, and adherence to a specific set of principles and ideals. In the creation of organizations, the organizational eagle is the entrepreneur. In the maintenance of organizations, the organizational eagle is the strategic planner, the organizational development professional, or the adherer to a discipline. Regarding change within organizations, the eagle is the long-range transformation planner. In the case of mergers, he or she focuses on ensuring a positive future for the employees. The organizational eagle believes in justice and equity for all parties. He or she looks for strategies that successfully impact the lives of all involved, and focuses toward collaborative solutions, the consensus win.

This is not to say that the eagle is without predatory instincts, rather that the eagle recognizes the possibilities but chooses the path that allows all to thrive. He or she strives to maintain the balance of nature, the balance of the organization. Being an eagle is the best option.

THE INTEGRITY OPTION

Individuals, organizations, and societies resort to violence because they do not confront and create strategies to solve fundamental ethical questions in their personal, organizational, and social lives. Three factors are significant in describing problems that influence ethical choice. Each factor focuses on ambivalence and frames current strategies for trying to answer ethical questions. The three factors are: (1) the appearance standard; (2) the rules standard; and (3) the practice standard. Each will be discussed more comprehensively in this section. It is important to recognize that discussions on ethics, ethical breeds, and the integration of breeds in performance are based on appearance, rules, and practice. To create a prescription to cure the violence within organizations requires an understanding of the standards that guide organizational choice.

In striving to be ethical, we must recognize that it is acceptable not to have all the answers to every question, issue, challenge, change, or new experience. Organizational business, change, and growth and the traditional issues of cost, production/service, and staffing must not be shortchanged by a fear of uncertainty. If uncertainty provides the window of opportunity to create rather than react, then it provides the best chance for reexamination of an organization's choices, policies, directions, and actions toward clients, employees, and the marketplace. The embracing of uncertainty becomes the first step toward evaluating the integrity issue.

The Burning Issue: Fear versus the Loss of Control

The issue of uncertainty is mired in two questions, both of which are caught up in the three standards of ethics or what can also be defined as the three standards of management within organizations: appearance, rules, and practice. These questions are: Is uncertainty based on one's *fear of the risk* of reaching out to embrace change or flexibility? Or is uncertainty based on the *inability to maintain control* in the face of change or flexibility? The issues of fear and control define the posturing that occurs among managers and employees within organizations. Further

questions arise when we confront these issues. Can we effectively address problems of diversity, growth management, product changes,
training, or human resource development without addressing the issues
of uncertainty that exist within the organization? Can we risk being
creative or effective if we are unwilling to challenge the uncertainty
existing within the corridors and halls of the executive suites? Will I
move to the beat of my own drum if I struggle with thoughts of losing
control to others by risking responding to choices that might usurp
tradition and history? Will we risk choosing a cohesive and collaborative
path to problem resolution, or will we detach, close up, distance, coerce,
and control in order to be comfortable? Will we choose calm through
action, or will we create violence through nonaction?

When a person or organization becomes mired in fear, four primary,
defensive stances begin to occur. Jack Gibb in his book *Trust: A New
View of Personal and Organizational Development* (Los Angeles: Guild of
Tutor Press, 1978) describes these fear-related behaviors that impact
personal and organizational functioning (Table 2.2): (1) depersoning, (2)
masking, (3) oughting, and (4) depending. These stances constitute a
defending process that impacts the orientation of the person with particular attention to the personal needs. The depersoning process looks
at coding and detaching defensive positions that lead to punishment as
a primary personal need. The masking process focuses on closing up,
distancing, filtering, covering, and strategizing behaviors. Within this
process, the personal need is distance to protect and manage actions
and experiences that enter one's personal space. The oughting process
focuses on influencing, persuading, parenting, coercing, and manipu-
lating as the primary defensive processes that impact action and thought.
The personal need here is to influence or to manage motives. The depending process focuses on control, submission, leading, domination,
and rebellion, with control as the personal need outcome. For Gibb,
these stances potentially define the processes that guide human and
organizational functioning. Each leads the person and the organization
to define a role, build a facade, discover one's needs, and control oneself
and others. Thus, each is a process of personal and organizational
destruction.

Integrity is significantly skewed when a person or organization operates from fear and control parameters. Motivation, consciousness, perception, emotionality, cognition, action, and synergy all become
aberrations. For example, in the movie *Altered States*, the human being
was continually in pain and torment for the lack of definition, clarity of
purpose, and wholeness—a lack of holism meant no future. Such is the
case for organizations and persons confronted with new options or new
perspectives on functioning. Fear and control create a lack of holism
and, thus, violence.

Table 2.2
The TORI (Trust, Openness, Risking, Interdependence) Defending Process

DEFENDING PROCESS	ORIENTATION OF THE PERSON	DEFENSIVE ENERGY FOCUSED ON:	PERSONAL NEEDS
DEPERSONING Coding Role-ing Detaching Appraising Observing	*Finding a role* Discovering and creating a role; What is my role? How do I compare with others?	*Punishing self and others* Evaluation Distrust Moralizing	*Punishment* Giving and receiving punishment Need to manage warmth
MASKING Closing up Distancing Filtering Strategizing Covering	*Building a facade* Discovering a strategy; How do I protect me? What is my best covert strategy?	*Strategizing* Circumvention Distortion Formality	*Distance* Giving and receiving social distance Need to manage intimacy
OUGHTING Influencing Persuading Parenting Coercing Manipulating	*Finding my needs* Discovering your demands and expectations; How do I change me or you? How do I get power?	*Persuading* Influence Passivity Resistance	*Influence* Giving and receiving influence Need to manage motives
DEPENDING Controlling Submitting Leading Dominating Rebelling	*Controlling me and you* Discovering rules, boundaries, contracts; How do I protect my turf? What is the law?	*Controlling* Dependency Management Rebellion	*Control* Giving and receiving controls Need to manage relationships

Source: Reprinted from Jack R. Gibb, *Trust: A New View of Personal and Organizational Development* (Los Angeles: Guild of Tutor Press, 1978), with permission.

CONCLUSION

If we are to expunge violence from our organizational and personal processes, we need to assess the strength within persons and organizations that allow us to embrace our ambivalence, integrity, and ethics, for only through exploring these areas can we grasp the challenges and the responsibilities inherent in changing violence and creating a different prescription for guiding organizational and personal functioning.

3

_____

Understanding the Process of Violence: Recognizing Our Participation

The process of violence is insidious in its creeping into our personal and professional lives. We become so intent on the outcomes of our plans that we miss the impacts of our many actions on others. In this chapter we look at how movement from control over others to influence with others occurs.

"Snow City," Texas, hired a new management team last year. The City Council told the new city manager that a paradigm shift needed to occur culturally for the city. Specifically, the city management team was told to create a program that allowed for the empowerment of employees. The team determined that the city needed an overhaul if it was to achieve the requirements set forth by the City Council. Two primary requirements were necessary for the development of the new paradigm. First the structure of management decision making required that the organization begin to decentralize the decision-making process. The process needed to move from one of control by the City Management Office to a one of influence throughout the organization. Second, the city management team determined that it needed to find a new director of human resources, committed to the ideal of empowerment, community, influence, and trust. They conducted a nationwide search and hired Mary for this position. The city management team then held a strategic planning session with all fourteen department heads of the city. The mission of the organization became effective service delivery to the citizens through a trust-based organizational process that valued the inclusiveness of employees and citizens in the development of strategies for ensuring a premium quality of life for the city.

Within two months, it became apparent that a significant gap existed between the strategic mission of the organization and the operational process. The city management team directed the new human resources director to recruit and hire a director of employee and organizational development. Simultaneously, they implemented policies directed at ensuring that empowerment, decentralization, and inclusiveness would guide organizational decision making. The city management team believed that they were well on their way to changing the organizational culture.

Eight months later, the city management team decided to conduct an Employee Opinion Survey to gauge the emotional health of the organization. They were shocked at the findings:

1. Employees did not trust management.
2. The structure of the organization was tiered, making it hard for employees to make decisions and accomplish goals. Everything flowed from the top; everything felt controlled.
3. Employees were afraid of management, believing that management was vindictive.
4. Employees felt that politics guided all actions and that competence was not valued. Nepotism, favoritism, and unethical behavior seemed to be the standard operating procedures.
5. Circumvention of the rules and extreme resistance were the strategies of the day.

The most frustrating of all results from the survey were comments from the staff of the human resources department. They felt demoralized in their work; the director consistently called them incompetent and chastised them for their work, and did not communicate effectively with them, even though it appeared that she gave them no guidance. She appeared hostile, discounted their existence, and reiterated a desire for "her own staff." Information was not shared, leaving employees in the dark regarding what direction they were taking.

One of the employees took the risk of signing her name to the survey prompting a meeting with city management. City management met with the employee and discovered that the staff was demoralized, distant, detaching from the organization, and almost rebelling. City management called the director in and gave her an ultimatum regarding changes in her performance; yet they gave her the maximum raise on her performance review. Human resources staff discovered the raise and felt abandoned by the city management team. In fact, employees had heard the director say, "The staff was upset with me; however, my bosses gave me a 4 percent raise. I can't be doing that bad." The staff felt compelled either to acquiesce to the director, whom they had begun to hate, or to rebel in order to maintain their sanity.

The new chief of employee and organizational development shared with the city management team that a circle of control existed within the organization. In spite of management's desire to create a paradigm shift, a continuance of control was the norm within the organization. Miscommunication, inconsistency, incongruence, and mistrust were the norms within the organization. Politics, not competence, was the avenue for success, and everyone was I-oriented. Thus, an organization of violence was in existence. If a change was to occur, city management had to actively support and speak to the circle of control.

Theoretically, the concept of organizational violence appears easy to understand. Organizations portray one perspective to the world yet operate from another perspective that discounts and violates the original perspective. Practically, however, the problem of violence is harder to understand for managers, executives, boards of directors, or consultants. Take the concept of control versus influence. In organizations, an entire system of violence is perpetuated by the joint actions of people and systems. Organizations would like for employees to believe that the organizational system is trustworthy, consistent, congruent, competent, and focused toward valuing their input to create a better product or to provide a better service. Organizational managers state that their communication is clear, consistent, and focused to suggest a we-orientation to work. Yet anytime employees experience miscommunication, inconsistency, incongruence, politics, or actions focused on individualism, trust in the organization begins to wane. When employees begin to mistrust the organization, a control system is in effect.

Figure 3.1 depicts a control system that operates within organizations. Circles of influence and circles of control exist for the organization and for each individual throughout the participatory process within an organization. Organizations create a philosophical direction that describes the operational policy for the organization. Depending on the individual or group perspective of the board of directors, city council, or top management, for example, that policy perspective may focus on control within the organization or it may focus on influence.

Wherever the organizational policy describes inclusion, empowerment, the value of human beings, and collaboration as key values, the organization operates from a circle of influence. The circle of influence has as its primary tenets: clear communication; trust; consistent performance in policies and actions; congruence as the behavior of choice; competence as the guiding principle for work, promotability, and longevity; collaboration as the strategy for decisions; and group or "we"

Figure 3.1
Control System

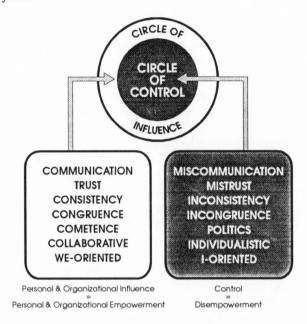

COMMUNICATION	MISCOMMUNICATION
TRUST	MISTRUST
CONSISTENCY	INCONSISTENCY
CONGRUENCE	INCONGRUENCE
COMETENCE	POLITICS
COLLABORATIVE	INDIVIDUALISTIC
WE-ORIENTED	I-ORIENTED

Personal & Organizational Influence
=
Personal & Organizational Empowerment

Control
=
Disempowerment

orientation. This philosophical direction should guide the hiring of managers, the development of policies and procedures, the ethical actions of employees, and the interaction of employees. This perspective should also guide the training of management for the future. The training program should adhere to the philosophical baseline perspectives denoted by these policies and procedures, establishing the framework for action. Should that occur, then the organization is congruent in its policy creation, hiring practices, and managerial and employee performance. Work is accomplished by persons who have all the necessary information to perform their roles. Each person receives a whole job that fosters reliance on his or her creativity. Each person recognizes the necessity for team-focused behavior based on a belief that all employees contribute to the effectiveness of the organization. Management supports inclusiveness because it expends substantial resources through training and development to ensure that all participants understand the values supported by the organization.

Conversely, the circle of control operates from a baseline perspective that sharing the power is not the desired outcome of the organization. Rather, fear keeps everyone in line or at least focused on the manipulation of others. The circle of control is based on the belief that only those at the top can be trusted, so decision making and authority are maintained at the top of the organization. Sharing of information becomes an anathema to control, therefore only enough information is shared to allow employees to perform tasks rather than whole jobs. Consistency defeats competition, therefore inconsistency becomes a key component of organizational action. Congruence is a fleeting thought in personal and organizational behavior, enhancing the likelihood of unethical behavior. Politics replaces competence as the strategy for promotability. Individualism replaces collaboration, and mistrust becomes the watchword for employees in their participation within the organization.

Both the circle of control and the circle of influence can operate successfully within organizations. However, one style commands a greater toll on employees and the organization than the other. One style embraces violence, whereas the other repels violence as defined in this book.

It is important to remember that violence is both a systemic and personal process. The systemic process focuses on the policies, procedures, and practices of the organization as well as the appearance, rules, and practice standards of the organization. The personal framework is based on the defending process of Jack Gibb's treatise in *Trust: A New View of Personal and Organizational Development*. Where there is lack of clarity within the organization, persons experience one or all of the defending processes described by Gibb; depersoning, masking, oughting, and depending become the orientations of protection for the individual. How does this occur? Usually, organizations are remiss in their definition of policies. What are shared with employees and most managers are the procedures and standard operating "policies" for everyday performance. Unfortunately, there are usually differences among groups within the organization. Let's say that an organization states that it values the creativity and participation of its employees—that their input helps the organization remain on the cutting edge. Promotions are based on ability to perform, and all employees are accorded equal opportunity to achieve, be recognized, and be valued. However, if the human resources department within that organization creates personnel policies and procedures that routinize work within the organization, creates rules that control and tie the hands of managers to stifle creativity for fear of violating laws and actions established by the department, and establishes multiple forms and regulations that require 40 percent of managers' time to comply with internal procedures reducing their potential to effectively lead their employees, then the human resources department is violating the premises of the organizational policy. If the human resources department forces managers to manage labor contracts as the management style of choice rather than lead people, then that department participates in the creation of violence within the organization. In that case, the human resources department is a purveyor of trauma, inconsistency, coercion, and detachment. The actions of the human resources department are diametrically opposed to the policies and rules of the organization.

The systemic or personal process of violence can manifest itself in many forms within an organization. An organization's finance department can create violence through its organizational structure. If it is hierarchically tiered, requiring all decision making to occur at the top of the organization, it defeats the purpose of encouraging decision making downward within the organization. Thus, employees do not believe the policies stated by management. A public works department can also be heavily tiered, suggesting that employees cannot be trusted to make sound decisions, thereby requiring action only at the top of the organization—another example of organizational violence. Yet another example is a chief operating officer who states at the annual employee luncheon that he is proud that employees are valued within the organization, yet the employees express their disbelief amongst themselves. What happened within these organizations was a mistrust of the policies based on practice and a violation of employees and of the organization. Employees did not believe that management was serious about its policies because management violated the policies in practice and structure. The more the organization tried to make employees believe they cared, the further employees moved from commitment to the organization because they mistrusted the words and actions of management. Management miscommunicated to employees through the dissonance existing between policies and practice. Management created a circle of control, not a circle of influence.

Two initial actions start the violence cycle. Figure 3.2 depicts two critical factors that impact violence. The first is the issue of systems and persons. When problems occur, we are quick to blame the individual for the actions that create problems rather than assessing whether the system is operating effectively. In actuality, almost 80 percent of problems that occur within organizations are created by the lack of effective functioning within the organizational system, whereas 20 percent are based solely on the dysfunctional actions of people. Every system is composed of policies, practices, and standards that express the focal energy of the system. Therefore, changes in the system can create issues and problems more than people can create problems. To determine that problem-oriented behavior is the primary fault of individuals discounts the accountability of the system for developing congruence in its policies and implementation strategies. Therefore, it is important to assesss the congruence of organizational action prior to leveling the dysfunction on people.

The second component of Figure 3.2 focuses on the expectation levels

Figure 3.2
The Imbalance Factors

SYSTEMS FOCUS

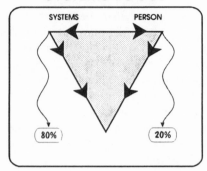

EXPECTATIONS CYCLE

that exist for individuals and organization policy. One's expectations are usually not shared with others, yet these expectations can be evident even when unspoken. As people pay more attention to nonverbal communication, they will pay more attention to expectation levels. We are quick to share expectations that are readily acceptable or easy to discuss. We are less ready to share those expectations that cause us to be more vulnerable. Therefore, approximately 80 percent of our expectations are implicit in nature or unshared while 20 percent of our expectations are explicit. It would be like the expectations we have of our spouses. Often we expect them to love, honor, and cherish us in the communal sense, but what we usually do not share is that we expect the other to protect and care for us as our parents have done. When spouses do not live up to that implicit expectation, we feel traumatized, discounted, and often violated. Unfortunately, our spouses have no idea why we feel violated because we neglected to share the expectation. The same is true in organizational life. Managers and employees often have expectations of each other that are implicitly based. Trauma occurs when the implicit expectation is violated; no information is shared to allow collaboration on the reasonableness of the expectation or the person's ability to follow through in meeting the expectation. Organizational policy provides a level of explicit expectation that often is violated when management chooses another path. Explicit expectations are violated when policies conflict; implicit expectations are violated when trust is impaired.

Let's look at how the process occurs. An organization creates a strategy for ensuring that all work is accomplished. It recognizes that people are essential to that success and establishes policies and frameworks for personal action within the boundaries of organizational life. In effect, the organization expects that everyone who works within the structure sees the world as the organization does. When the organization experiences that other world views exist, dysfunction begins to set in. Managers and supervisors within the organization do not understand why employees do not embrace changes in work scopes, assignments, or work partners on a project. Managers and supervisors believe that the organization makes its choice based on the changing parameters of the industry, the competition of like-minded firms, or the loss of revenue caused by changing dynamics within a state that uses taxes as the primary fund for city government revenue. Employees, however, often feel that changes are personal in nature, that management makes a change to ensure some level of profitability or political influence that is self-motivated. The needs or wants of the employee are forgotten in the process. The real issue is the level of arrogance displayed by the manager or the organization in the decision-making process.

Consider a deputy city manager, unfamiliar with the dynamics of training as an organizational system. The deputy city manager is accountable for the smooth administrative running of the organization. To be true to his accountability, the deputy city manager hoards the decision-making process. He reviews the language of memoranda, augments the decisions of department directors because they do not meet his view, changes the scopes of work dictated by the council because he thinks he knows best how to achieve the outcome, and holds up work by experts in different disciplines to ensure that his perspective is understood and conveyed in training classes. He believes he is upholding his accountability within the organization. He is disdainful of criticism for he believes that what he does is the correct thing to protect the City Council and the city manager. We can understand his need to protect and serve. Unfortunately, his perspective and approach are violent in a professional way. The processes of constant review, rewriting of memoranda, unilateral changing of work scope, and holding up work to ensure a certain perspective exists are all forms of organizational violence. The assumption that *"I know what is best"* is what creates the violence. No trust of experts, council, employees, managers, or supervisors exists, only the belief that the deputy manager's perspective is the right perspective. If that is the case, then all the persons he chooses to mistrust are no longer needed. In effect, doing what he believes is right violates the professionalism of all parties and emasculates the egos and sense of good will of all the people involved.

We revisit Snow City, Texas, to catch up on the results of the human resources director and the chief of employee and organizational development. The chief of employee and organizational development decided to resign. He cited as the reason for his decision the massive need for control on the part of the director of human resources. Mary had alienated all of her staff. She had controlled all work products without having expertise in any of the areas. She blindly followed the actions and style of the deputy city manager for administrative services. Her staff was kept in the dark until the last minute and then castigated for clerical errors in trying to meet very short time frames. She discounted the need for inclusiveness and common courtesy with her staff and violated personnel rules with disregard for the impacts created on the employees. Employees reporting directly to her were fearful to complain, believing that the deputy city manager would not listen or would violate confidences and that vindictiveness would become the pattern of action. The organization was unhealthy, and organizational violence continued to be the norm of existence. The desire for change appeared to be only an alteration of control. The chief decided that participation in the process was futile; another type of internal consultant was required. He thus extricated himself from the violence.

Numerous examples of this form of violence are evident in government, private industry, and nonprofit organizations. Everyday the existence of violence is rationalized or discounted. Situations continue to oppress and destroy the skills and abilities of employees and organizations to be effective. Everyday, people leave, hoping to fit better into another organization. Profit, power, control, politics, and self-indulgence become more entrenched as the strategy of organizational life. Thus, the violence continues.

Part Two

Four Cases of Organizational Violence

The next four chapters depict four different situations within organizations where it is believed that the organizations are responding appropriately to changing environments. Each situation represents a common aspect of today's organizational life. The first situation is the case of a health care research facility whose members perceive that change must occur. The facility's management believes strongly that change in the form of diversity must be embraced by the organization. On the part of the chief executive officer, frustration resulting from ten years of unresponsiveness has led to mandates, the implementation of which is assigned to the Department of Human Resources. The case focuses on the human resources director who tries to balance the needs of the CEO with the ability of his staff to make the shift from a maintenance-oriented personnel department to a full-fledged human resources department charged with being the instrument of change.

The second case involves the organizational violence that occurs when a city manager responds to the changing priorities of the city council. The council creates a change in organizational direction based on the first stages of a strategic planning process. The change is constricted by resources, forcing the city manager to dissolve a department. The violent struggle is the expunging of the department and the accompanying revelations of the staff caught in the reduction in force. The case focuses on the struggles of the employees to understand the change, and the management team's belief that they have responded to change in a humane and caring manner.

The third case addresses the issue of creating more profit. Northeast Test Preparation Center, a well-known educational preparation firm, has over the past ten years created an incentive program for its facility managers through the philosophy that more innovative work breeds more personal and corporate profit. A new crop of MBA graduates was hired to change the financing structure of the organization. In December 1992, Northeast Test Preparation Center placed its facility managers on salaries and altered the commission process, significantly reducing the incentive and morale of its facility managers. The case thus focuses on the impact of change for a facility manager and his perception of the organizational violence that has become a standard of the organization.

The fourth case is an examination of organizational violence in government, based on a cultural change involving work standards, work accountability, teamwork, and ethnic/gender issues. Southern California County is the geographically largest county (22,000 square miles) in the United States. The county has 15,000 employees. Facilities Management is one department in the Public Works Group. It is headed by a Latin American woman with thirty years of organizational experience. As she has grown professionally, she has struggled with balancing her beliefs about work with her emerging understanding of herself. This process has often placed her in the middle of balancing the needs of the organization with her expectations of staff. This has resulted in a struggle to change the organization and herself without creating violence. However, violence has abounded for her and her employees. The case focuses on her attempts to expunge the violence.

4

The Southwest Medical Research Center Challenge: Shifting the Role of Human Resources

Matt wakes up at 5:00 A.M. worried about a meeting with his chief executive officer (CEO). Matt is the human resources director for the Scottsdale, Arizona, facility of the Southwest Medical Research Center, the world's most well-known medical research center. He is worried because he has struggled for weeks with the concept of change within the organization. The CEO has been with the Southwest Medical Research Center for over ten years, but six months ago, he came to the Scottsdale facility to take over the reins of an expanding research arm of the parent agency. The CEO stated upon his arrival that change must occur in the diversity of the organization's personnel. Matt strategically looked at approaches for changing the visual makeup of the organization. He recognizes that the current makeup violates the system standard of diversity stated in the organizational mission; however, he recognizes that the organizational structure is two-tiered with regard to power and authority. The CEO is one leader, the physicians' group the other. Irrespective of the CEO's wishes, the physicians make up the decision-making tier of the organization. Matt does not believe that racism is a part of the decision-making process, rather that history has unknowingly locked the physicians into recruiting in only one fashion: Hire someone who *fits*. Matt knows that this means that the tendency is to hire whites, thereby making his job harder.

As Matt prepares for his meeting, he thinks over the strategies he has put together. However, he is not sure that the CEO will listen. The CEO is adamant about change occurring within the organization, and Matt is committed as well; yet Matt believes timing is essential to a successful outcome. In discussing the merits of the issue with Matt, a friend who is a consultant challenged his perspective of timeliness as a cop-out for instituting change. Matt found himself struggling with the concept of personal values and organizational need.

At the start of the meeting, the CEO reiterates his commitment to changing the face of the organization and now places a restriction. The CEO states that no hiring will occur unless the prospective employee is nonwhite or female. Matt struggles with that directive because he recognizes that the organization will be put at risk. He works furiously to create a strategy to carry out the CEO's wishes, discusses his strategy with the legal counsel, and makes an appointment for both to see the CEO.

The CEO is frustrated. He had joined the Scottsdale facility of the Southwest Medical Research Center for its ability to risk taking on hard challenges, and diversity inclusion is a hard challenge. The Southwest Medical Research Center decision makers had discussed the issue for years, creating commitment to inclusiveness as a part of its mission and committing funds for training and development of its employees; yet, the Scottsdale clinic was not making a lot of movement in the area. There had been some key appointments of minorities and women but no substantial change. Did it mean that the research center wasn't really committed to diversity? Or did it mean that the center just didn't know how to embrace difference? Were people within the organization trying to sabotage the mission? Was he the only one really committed to change? He trusts Matt. Matt has a background of consistency, compassion, and congruence; he graduated from a Quaker school, has a background in organizational behavior, and was a member of the Peace Corps in Africa. Certainly he understands. However, the CEO wants Matt to move faster and harder. He thinks, "Maybe he needs to know that I support him."

Matt and Nancy, the legal counsel, meet with the CEO. They discuss the pluses and minuses of the CEO's directive, offer an alternative, and get assurances from the CEO to try a different tact. Matt realizes in his struggle that the organizational system must be altered. The Southwest Medical Research Center Scottsdale Clinic values data as critical to effective decision making. The human resources system of the organization lacks data. His staff operates from knowledge of the history of the organization, not data within the organization. Without data, it will be hard to alter the perspectives of the physician decision makers. Thus, a change must occur in the human resources system, which becomes Matt's mission. His goal is not to hire new employees, but to enhance the skills of the existing staff quickly in order for them to expand their vision of the field of human resources, their own skills, and their role within the organization.

The human resources staff is made up of three professional analysts and two technical professionals. Each feels that he or she entered the field of human resources by accident, but they have found the field rewarding because of the work they have performed and the recruitment processes that have yielded good candidates for positions.

The statement by the CEO has made the human resources staff very uncomfortable. They have to work in the organizational environment, and they must get along with the physician decision makers. They feel it is unfair for the CEO to ask them to work harder, differently, and without clearer guidelines. They understand the Southwest Medical Research Center system and feel that there is no real *organizational* push for this change. This is a violation of all they understand about the nature of the work. Trauma sets in. Matt had brought in a consultant who they feel accused them of being perpetuators of this bad system. He challenged their integrity and their professionalism. He asked them to consider working in teams because their style of relating often involved giving in to or being afraid of the physician decision makers. How dare he violate their professionalism, challenge their skills, and suggest that they did not have the data to be influential! Matt had participated in this process; what did he really think of them? Matt had worked hard to build a cohesive team; how could he do this to them? They feel violated, emotionally attacked, professionally stifled.

The issues raised in this case are the same issues for hundreds of human resources systems in all types of organizations around the country. The particular issue in this case focuses on how to move a human resources department through a paradigm shift without experiencing violence. Without getting into my strategic system for resolving organizational violence, it might be helpful to explore the violence parameters generated by this case. In chapter one, I state that the tenets of violence are: (1) the inability of people and organizations to create bonds that foster collaboration and inclusiveness; (2) inclusiveness by organizational leaders to involve all in understanding the outcomes of the organization; (3) the inability of leaders to balance the need for individuality with the work ethic of the team; (4) embracing rather than discounting the introduction of ideals and ideas; (5) resolving issues of control, power, and authority; and (6) the inability to assess life's dichotomies where choices are made regarding ends justifying the means versus the means as a critical dynamic toward achieving an appropriate and just end. In the case of the Scottsdale facility of the Southwest Medical Research Center, organizational success must be balanced by the health of the employees and the organizational congruence of policies, procedures, and practices with desired outcomes. Has the organization done enough to ensure that no violence will occur with the change of a policy, procedure, or practice dealing with diversity? In this case, the answer is no.

It is important to remember that none of the organizations discussed in this book has intentionally created violent strategies. Yet the process of violence has inevitably existed because little attention has been paid to expunging the tenets of organizational violence. The Southwest Medical Research Center clinic's process of bonding focuses on a one-way process of joining. The tenets of the organization as expressed in its mission statement suggest inclusiveness as a very high value. The mission statement says, "To realize the vision, Southwest Medical Research Center commits itself (1) to be a unified medical system, (2) to recruit and retain outstanding people to work as a team in an interdisciplinary setting, (3) to promote cultural diversity and equality of opportunity within the Southwest Medical Research Center family, (4) to respect the individual contributions of each member. . . . " The tenets speak to respecting the differences of individuals and working toward inclusiveness and diversity. The appearance of the Southwest Medical Research Center staff suggests that only whites are valued by the organization in its hiring practice. There is no visible evidence in the marketing and annual literature of the facility that persons of color are valued or respected by the organization. Bonding in this case becomes a process of homogeneity in looks. As the director of human resources reviews the value system of his staff, it becomes apparent that persons of like-minded views are valued and that inclusion of persons of differing perspectives could create a process of exclusion from the organization. Inclusiveness is not valued when viewing growth within the organization. The third tenet of violence speaks to individuality as a balance for effective teamwork. When everyone looks and thinks the same, it is difficult for balance to occur, so the director begins to wonder about the issue of groupthink. If everyone thinks alike, works hard to view the Southwest Medical Research Center world the same way, and works toward homogeneity, maybe it is impossible to achieve a real balance. Effectually, instituting inclusiveness in Southwest Medical Research Center might create a real process of violence.

The CEO of the Southwest Medical Research Center, Scottsdale facility, is confronted with the issue of embracing inclusion and change versus exclusion and history. The movement from one to the other is a process of violence because little care has been taken to inform members of the organization about the necessity for change. The lack of inclusion creates violence in the existing systems. There are no levels of standards that seem to move toward inclusion or resolution of historical control, power, or authority standards. The concept of standards for the organizational system seems not to exist, although medical standards, analysis standards, and function standards are in place. At Southwest

Medical Research Center, everything appears to function to serve the physicians. Therefore, the ends may justify the means. For example, getting the right research result may require groupthink. Altering the culture or creating a paradigm shift may cause more violence than achieving the mission of inclusion and diversity. The organizational history has set the stage for violence because the organization does not adhere to its principles and values. Ten years of talking about change supports the last tenet of violence—that choices are made regarding ends justifying the means versus the means are a critical dynamic toward achieving an appropriate and just end.

Matt must analyze the data he is discovering as a part of his desire to expunge violence. This assessment is different from determining appropriate training within the organization, establishing new recruitment strategies for inclusion, or upgrading the skills of his staff. This analysis focuses on the success of a paradigm shift within the organization. He asks himself the questions: Can change occur without destroying the organization? Is the organization ready to value diversity as much as it values physicians' preference? Can staff respond to the many frustrations involving inclusiveness as they respond to medical excellence? Is change worth the violence? Will too much trauma be the outcome, and are the means worth the just and appropriate end?

Look at the focus of this discussion. It is settling on the concept of violence as the key factor. Traditionally, management analysis would look at the overall mission of the organization and determine that the appropriate approach would involve building a balance or congruence between the missions and beliefs of the organizations with the actions of the players within the organization. If that were sufficient, then Matt, as human resources director, would begin to build more structure within the organization to ensure that less flexibility would create violations to the mission. Policies, procedures, and administrative regulations would become the dictating factor for success. The physicians are not participating in a covert attempt to thwart diversity; they believe that they understand and know the best approach essential to effective research—research and the best fit are best for the organization. Marvin Weisbord's six box process (*Organizational Behavior: An Applied Psychological Approach* [Dallas: Hammer and Organ, 1978]) would suggest that rewards, environment, and other factors are in place. Compensation is good, equipment and environment are excellent, and the organization is effectively moving forward toward its mission. Certainly the process of change is slow, however; incremental change is mandated because all other components of the organizational system are in place. Kurt Lewin's Force Field Analysis (*Organizational Communication: The Essence of Effective Management*, 2nd ed. [Columbus, OH: Phillip Lewis Grid Publishers, 1980]) suggests that the organizational culture did not demand change. The congruence system described in my book *The Congruence of People and Organizations* (Westport, CT: Quorum Books, 1993) suggests that management wants change without a real balance between the beliefs and needs of employees. More important, the human resources staff operates from a predominantly legal belief system suggesting that power, authority, and control are critical factors. Embracing diversity sets the stage for dissonance and discomfort. Little experience with diversity breeds a loss of control, power, and authority. In effect, none of the traditional approaches to understanding dysfunction would prepare the human resources department or the CEO for the creation of ineffective structures.

To make a difference, Matt would have to struggle with a new analysis process—a nonviolent prescriptive approach. Matt would have to begin his analysis with an evaluation of all six tenets of violence. Does each tenet exist within the organization? Have the tenets influenced the organizational functioning where disagreements have generated impasses, work slowdowns, or work discounts? Would employees describe a process of abandonment, noncommitment, and disrespect from management in its attempt to embrace a new issue? Has the bonding requirement been violated? Have employees been directed to be inclusive, or have they chosen to participate in the creation of inclusion? The extent to which employees feel excluded is the extent to which employees retreat and build strategies for protection. This would be extremely true of the physicians and all other employees who trust the organization's pledge to promote from within. When the organization states that diversity/ equity is valued above equality, employees struggle with individualism versus the team concept. They have worked hard to get where they are, and diversity is an unknown and an untested variable.

Each of these factors becomes critical as a component of analyzing violence within the organization. The outcome desired is the creation of a strategy that balances organizational needs with employee needs. The employees trust the organization's pledges. Violation of that trust creates violence. Traditional methods of evaluation, therefore, never approach the violence quotient.

Southwest Medical Research Center, Scottsdale facility, discovers that experiencing the violence is a part of the paradigm shift—not that it has to be, rather that nonadherence to the values of the mission create a violent atmosphere forcing explosions as a part of the change. Matt and his staff have their work cut out for them. The challenge is not in the traditional management strategies for change; the challenge is in working toward rebuilding and restructuring all the violations that occur. Each of the tenets of violence must be repaired. Starting with bonding, the human resources department must organizationally guide the rebuilding of bonds between employees and the organization. Human resources must begin to ensure that all growth and change in the future are inclusively oriented, not exclusively decided by a few to impact the whole. The department must create programs and strategies that balance individual effort with team service. It must become the champion of embracing ideas and ideals, and it must guide the empowerment of the organization to be comfortable with present and future expansion. Finally, human resources will have shifted its role when it recognizes that means are dynamic experiences that move toward the achievement of appropriate and just ends.

5

Central City Challenge: Downsizing for the Future

"Central City" has embarked on a strategic planning process for managing all work of the city. This is the second year it has been in effect. During the review of issues, the City Council adopted a new mission and guiding principles describing how the organization would approach all issues. In the review process, five key objectives for fiscal year 1993–1994 were adopted by the council. The objectives identified a significant shift in work scope that might create a problem for the existing organizational structure. The shift involves a larger emphasis on affordable housing, community redevelopment versus downtown redevelopment, significant enhancement of transportation and circulation issues, acceptance and implementation of the Multijurisdictional Empowerment Commission, and public works maintenance/infrastructure issues.

The city administration recognizes that budgetary restraints make it difficult to maintain the current organizational structure while shifting focus to affordable housing, citywide redevelopment, and transportation. Most of the required skills are unavailable, suggesting a change is needed in organizational structure. City administration wants to ensure that change can occur to implement council needs without "busting" the budget. Over a two-month period, discussions ensue leading to the decision to eliminate the Design and Development Department, to create an Office of Architectural Services within the Public Works Department, to use the savings to hire a housing expert and a transportation planner, and to implement the Multijurisdictional Empowerment Commission results in the minority community of Central City.

Ted is the division chief of project control in the Design and Development Department. Rumor has it his department is being eliminated from the city. Ted, though nervous, believes that his role is secure. The city will always have remodeling projects, and numerous projects are still underway requiring the project control that he provides for the city.

Paul, director of Design and Development, comes to work amid feelings of loss, trepidation, anger, and frustration. It is his duty to inform his department that they are being eliminated. The hardest task he has is sharing with the division chiefs that their services are no longer required, as they are included in the reduction in force. There is slight consolation in Paul's belief that the organization has been caring in the process because six-month severance is being allowed. Paul worries that the division chiefs will be angry.

Paul meets with the staff to relate the bad news. He states that Design and Development is no longer a department and that the Office of Architectural Services is being created. Nine staff members are being let go, and eight will be retained in the new division reporting to the city engineer. Feelings are tense; some employees cry, others curse, and still others say this is impossible. Questions abound: How was the selection made? Who is responsible for the change? We are good employees; we have fixed mistakes that have saved the city money. How can they get rid of us and keep the screw-ups? Paul's frustration is heightened. He calls the Human Resources Department for help.

The employees beat him to Human Resources. They want answers. "What are my rights? Am I eligible to be returned to the Classified Service? Will you provide outplacement services? What about career testing, resumé development, time for interviewing?" Human Resources says that they have no answers; they were brought into the process late. The employees are more frustrated. They want justice. Paul wasn't powerful enough. There needs to be some balance here. "We need to band together and fight this thing. I know there is something wrong. How can they get rid of the most talented people within the department and keep the less talented?"

Central City is experiencing a violent reaction to a perceived caring act toward the Department of Design and Development. Management believes it had saved its own neck by gracefully eliminating a department. The decision was based on the actions of the City Council, and management had carefully reviewed all the departments to make the decision that was handed down to the employees. The decision was a unilateral act on the part of management. Employees, on the other hand, perceive the actions of management as a political ploy, wrought with innuendos that are uncaring, punitive, and unfair. How did this level of dissonance occur? What were the issues between management and employees that were missed in the decision-making process, and how did these issues arise?

The analysis of problems traditionally focuses on the inherent issues of structure, policy, procedure, costs, direction, and people. Unfortunately, the analysis is based on the historical revelations managers have about the issue of change. In this situation, the City Council dictates the parameters of change, moving from capital improvement projects to infrastructure repair. Focus is placed on issues the council believes best meet the needs of the community. Based on those parameters, decisions are made that focus on building a structure to match the expressions of the council. Policy choices move toward redevelopment, transportation, and multicultural inclusion processes. Organizational procedures are followed for insuring that change is orderly, within bargaining and personnel rules, and that costs are allocated to display caring toward the employees in the restructure process. The direction is set, and management moves forward in a caring manner.

It doesn't work; the changes do occur, but they are perceived as volatile and destructive. What is not caring about the process? Exclusion of affected persons is the beginning of the violence process. Management needs to look at the desired outcome: saving money while changing focus of the organization. There are myriad avenues one can use to save money and change the focus of an organization. In this case, change needs to be balanced by weighing people and systems equally. The lack of balance in this case creates a *balance of power* situation within the organization. Employees believe that fairness is not the guiding principle—politics is. Employees who consistently produce low-quality work and service are kept within the organization; employees within the department who have political ties, not technically specific skills, are kept for the Office of Architectural Services. Employees who have the credentials and certifications and those who speak their minds about what would be effective irrespective of political intent were let go. Power, not fairness, is the perceived controller. Because of power, employees feel that they must *balance the power* by publicly pointing out the error of management's decisions. Employees speak to other employees to create fear that their organizations will be eliminated next. Employees write letters to City Council members, expressing their dismay at the decision-making process. Employees look at strategies to involve the unions, creating power checks and associations of freedom, believing that numbers equal power. Overall, the employees have a different view than management—political decision making is the end result of the organizational change. In effect, what management believed was a fair and equitable process is discounted by employees as a continual process of fear within the organization. The cycle of violence begins to grow; management feels attacked, and employees feel abused. Both sides are right; both sides become pitted against each other. Central City is in the throes of violence.

Ted reviews his frustration with the events of the organization. Ted can either accept the actions of the organization and devote energy toward the creation of options that maximize his strengths, or he can use up his energy being frustrated and fighting against the actions of the organization. Unfortunately, many persons experiencing dissonance with organizational decision making create volatile and violent strategies to check the power of organizations or compete against organizations.

In the case of downsizing, organizations effectively discount their ability to affect employees positively. The process of creating change for the good of the organization without looking at the options and opportunities for the employee initializes *incongruous competition* into the equation. Defeat is the outcome. Managers rationalize their actions, employees chastise the organization, and everyone loses. Groupthink and group control are the outcomes for the organization, discounting the values of the individual.

The ethical breeds described in chapter two come into play here. The issues of this case suggest that the organization wants the employees of the Design and Development Department to be "antelopes," as are the managers—consummate team players. The organizational antelope wants everyone to accept the outcome of change as best for the work group or organization. The antelope wants harmony and agreement to ensure blending into the organization. Ted and the other managers are operating from the "lion" perspective. They believe that the management team has not acted with courage or ethics. This means that management lacks honor in its use of politics, and the lion looks on this behavior with disdain. A larger beast—unethical politics—must be attacked; consummate skills, the mark of the lion, must be allowed to overcome.

To the managers, a level of honesty needs to occur. Someone within management needs to operate from the stance of the "eagle." The decision might be more readily accepted if ethics and excellence are visibly valued. To the managers, no waste exists within their department. They have consistently performed well, and their dedication to excellence has been discounted and shunned for unethical reasons. The organization could no longer be trusted, and the management team is the purveyor of mistrust. In effect, the integrity options—the appearance, rules, and practice standards—are violated in the eyes of the employees. The organization takes a defending position of *masking*, whereas the employees experience closing up, distancing, strategizing, and covering.

The managers are trapped; they bought into a process of defensiveness without realizing the consequences. The managers begin to create *de-*

pending processes. Controlling, submitting, dominating, and rebelling approaches become the visible actions, and the rules, boundaries, and contracts are the outcomes that employees see. Management works not for inclusion or acceptance but to create control and dominance. The organizational lions, the managers of Design and Development, are hooked into Jack Gibb's defending processes (*Trust: A New View of Personal and Organizational Development* [Los Angeles: Guild of Tutor Press, 1978]).

The deputy city manager of Community Development recognizes that the perceived outcome did not occur. He decides to talk with the employees affected by the decision to eliminate the department. He recognizes that anger and frustration would be a major component of what he would hear; however, he knows that a change to a more positive approach would not occur without clearing the air. The employees are scared. The city had given them a nice severance package, but they believe that they need to function as lions and eagles. As lions, they want to let the deputy understand their frustration and anger with the decision; as eagles, they want to express to the deputy what they believe is right.

The meeting is very tense. The deputy becomes defensive and wants to create control. He does not want the meeting to get out of hand. The employees listen to his rationale, become more frustrated and angry with his control tactics, and proceed to rebel. Within ten minutes, the deputy and the managers are not listening; they become entrenched in their positions. Everyone loses.

It is hard to be in a position of authority, tasked with making decisions, trapped in maintaining an organizational position, frustrated with the impact a decision has on others, yet determined to be the organizational antelope. It is also hard to be on the receiving end of frustration and comply with statements made for the "good of the organization." In such cases, one feels violated, hurt, and discounted and that bonding with the company had not occurred. The tenets of violence come into play. One becomes a victim of the groupthink and group control processes, of the defending processes, and, ultimately, of organizational violence. One understands all the management philosophies of trust, communication, conflict resolution, inclusion, competence, and collaboration, as well as the two dynamics of fear and loss. Thus, fear and loss become the overriding drivers for one's action.

What happened in Central City is common. How the managers and administrative team responded and how the violence occurred is the norm. How the cycle gets broken is a different approach, however.

Ted begins to look at his opportunities. He still smarts from the actions of the organization and continues to believe that the organization only values its needs. Concern for him as an outstanding manager are discounted. Ted feels that he cannot trust working for others. Devoting time, energy, and commitment have hurt him too significantly to go through it again. Ted begins to research his options as a developer and architect. He is certain that he will perform much differently with persons who work with him. His opportunities look great; he is prepared, and he chooses to operate as the organizational eagle. Luck needs to be his constant companion, for it is easy to fall into the traps of violence.

The deputy city manager also learns from the experience. He recognizes that the change required is both organizational and personal, thus both levels must be considered in contemplating change. He is trapped by the inability of his breed—the antelope—to recognize and influence the tenets of violence. He is trapped by his own defending process and the defending processes of everyone he meets.

One other critical point: The organization may not recover. Every instance of violence begets an additional wall that inhibits collaboration and trust. Should change occur within the organization in the future, there may be less opportunity for everyone to win. The balance of power, freedoms of association, and incongruous competitions have become set in stone. The unions abound, nonparticipation is the norm for fear that one may get trapped into past practices without recognizing the impact on the individual, and unresolved violence still lingers. Continuing to address issues from traditional management strategies is not working. Combining traditional strategies with strategies for expunging violence may be the only option.

6

Profit Enhancement: The MBA Crunch at Northeast Test Preparation Center

David was managing the Manhattan facility of an educational test preparation corporation for six years. During that time, he had watched sales increase by 36 percent. He felt proud of the increase, and he believed that his approach to quality, quantity, and service had been the deciding factor. It appears that his belief was shared by the management of the organization. His salary had gone from $65,000 to $158,000 in the six years, accompanied with a title change from office manager to general manager of the Manhattan facility. In the process, David had worked hard to ensure that his staff had been taken care of. Their salaries had increased 35 percent, and his contracted faculty had enjoyed substantial increases as well.

The corporation appears to have profited substantially by his managerial and business acumen, even though this was not his first professional career choice. Management had continually praised him for his work, flexibility, and critical thinking style that appears to have allowed him to create new marketing and management strategies. Management even suggested to him that he take a promotion within the organization that would place him just below the glass ceiling of executive-level management. David thought long and hard about the option and discussed it with his wife in terms of their long-range goals. He finally decided that it would make more sense to present a different option to management.

David felt that the real profit incentives lay with the outlying facilities of the corporation. For as long as he could remember, the real income was generated by the incentives given facility managers outside New York. The company had always stated, "Create a plan that works, generate sales beyond your targets, and your commission checks will yield 25 percent beyond your salaries for all income generated beyond the targets." David had watched his peers earn income beyond the wildest dreams of the corporation. Salaries and commissions for some facility managers were close to $350,000 per year, even with a base of $100,000. David spoke with the Chief Executive Officer (CEO) and the Chief Operating Officer (COO) about his thoughts. The North Carolina facility near Duke University was performing poorly. He believed that his marketing techniques and the work he exhibited in New York would truly turn that facility around, generating significant profits for the organization. He told management that his approach could recoup corporate losses within twelve months and increase sales by an additional 31 percent during the next twelve months. He created a business plan for their review detailing the scope of his approach and some of the strategies he could employ to achieve the results desired by the corporation. The CEO and COO were very impressed with his plan. They approved it, and David was off to North Carolina.

This was extremely important for David. His entire family seemed to be migrating from the northeast in favor of the Carolinas. This move was a value-added process for his entire family. David would be able to spend quality time with family and friends; his wife would be able to create designs for a custom home that they had always wanted; and David would be able to put into practice ideas of management and profit generation that he had thought about for six years—a perfect marriage of values and work ethics.

Within six weeks, David and his wife had moved to North Carolina. It was around the holidays, and David knew that this was a slow time in the business. This would give him the opportunity to significantly plan for the changes he was about to make within the organization. As he began to peruse the possibilities over Christmas week, he was mortified; it was worse than he thought, but not insurmountable. He knew he could make a difference, and so he began.

Within six months, things were looking up. He had streamlined the organizational structure, built relationships with the universities in the area, surveyed the potential market, and determined that more work could be done in the Medical College Aptitude Test (MCAT) and the Law School Aptitude Test (LSAT). The Graduate Management Aptitude Test (GMAT) was the bread and butter of the corporation in this area, and he would ensure that the corporation's share of the market would remain high.

Even though these activities were occurring, David had heard some disturbing news about changes in the New York office. A new crop of management types were entering the organization. The *Washington Post* had obtained controlling interest in the corporation and had begun to bring in Harvard MBAs to make system and policy changes. It was clear that these new people were out to make names for themselves. They were making changes very quickly that they believed were impacting the bottom line of the organization. David, however, was not too worried. He was in an outlying facility, and the contractual arrangement for profit and commission seemed safe. David continued on his business plan, making changes and increasing sales. He felt that his ideas were working well.

By the end of the following year, things had begun to change. The national office had changed, and new approaches to salary and commission were being instituted by the new MBA crowd. David talked with his counterparts around the country, most of whom were upset about the new changes in approach to compensation. The changes were affecting their long-range plans for compensation and retirement planning. The organization was reneging on their agreements, and they were the ones being hurt by this change. The parent corporation was being greedy, and the changes appeared to be a real value shift within the organization. David was worried. He liked the organization historically because the founder valued people. He had always worked from the perspective that profit would grow if people were valued in the process. People would work harder and produce more when they felt included in choices and changes. This entire organizational perspective was being violated, and, thus, changes were occurring in the people.

For example, the outlying facility managers were changing. In the past, they were energized, hopeful, enjoined with the organization, and included in the long-range organizational plans that would impact the future of the organizational system and the people. Trust, collaboration, inclusiveness, and teamwork were historical beliefs that guided the organization. This new crop of MBAs had instituted, in a unilateral manner, a new organizational culture. David felt that this was a bad omen. However, he would adopt a wait-and-see attitude, hoping that the changes would not significantly affect him and his facility.

David was wrong. Near the end of December, the organization presented him with a new profit incentive plan. It was more of a disincentive plan. It raised his targets, reduced the support from the parent organization, and cut his commission structure in half. David was trapped. He began to rationalize the structure change, saying, "At least I have a commission structure; a lot of peers have only a salary now, and it has been cut significantly." David no longer trusted the parent organization. It was violating everything it had ever valued.

David's plight is typical of the situations played across the country in organizations bent on changing profits for the good of the organization.

It appeared to David and many others that the concept of partnership was no longer viable. Only issues of profit and loss—the bottom line— were valued by the organization in its desire to change the face and structure of organizational life. Although the new crop of MBAs at Northeast Test Preparation Center had changed the bottom line, it was not in the way they had thought. Overall profits from the outlying facilities were down 18.5 percent; changes in management of the out- lying facilities were occurring; increased communication between the remaining managers was increasing; disgruntlement and mistrust were increasing throughout the organization; and the old values of inclusion, collaboration, teamwork, and trust were waning. What had emerged in this process was the creation of organizational violence.

Some theorists would posture that the policies of the Reagan and Bush administrations in the 1980s caused this type of organizational change. Others would assert that the 1980s and early 1990s unleashed a ground- swell of unethical management and organizational practice. Some would say that management is doing the right thing, that waste in capital caused the change. New management in organizations has realized that greater profits are possible and has acted on the information to achieve greater organizational profits. Still others would say that management has begun to reap the fruits of discounting human resources within organizations. I would pose a different theory.

In this book, organizational violence is an underlying issue of analysis, but it is usually disregarded in approaches to assessing the health and wealth of an organization. Usual approaches include Demming's four- teen points of organizational health and change, Marvin Weisbord's six box theory of organizational analysis (*Organizational Behavior: An Applied Psychological Approach* [Dallas: Hammer and Organ, 1978]), Kurt Lewin's force field analysis (*Organizational Communication: The Essence of Effective Management*, 2nd ed. [Columbus, OH: Phillip Lewis Grid Publishers, 1980]), Jack Gibb's trust theory matrix (*Trust: A New View of Personal and Organizational Development* [Los Angeles: Guild of Tutor Press, 1978]) and my congruence/belief analysis (*The Congruence of People and Organizations* [Westport, CT: Quorum Books, 1993]). Each of these approaches allows one to get pieces of the puzzle regarding this case identified. Demming would say that management at Northeast Test Preparation Center cre- ated an aura of noncreation. The approaches of management choked the creative potential of the line managers. Gibb would expand on that thought, stating that fear was created within the organization by man- agers posturing issues of protectionism. This protectionism reduced the energy necessary for creation of productive work because trust was violated and depersoning occurred. Lewin would suggest that the cor- poration, in its inception of change, violated the principles of change. Freezing of the organizational culture, necessary for change to be embraced, did not occur. Weisbord would say that lack of assessing the tenets of organizational change allowed management to disregard the importance of rewards as a critical factor of the organization's success.

According to my belief systems theory, the organization in its inception was of a psychological/legal belief structure, implying that empowerment and inclusiveness of employees in decision making were necessary for success. Managers who were originally hired matched the belief structure of the organization, and success abounded. When the MBAs altered the organizational belief structure, management possessing belief systems consistent with the change was not in place to accept and ensure compliance with the belief changes. This created a gap between the values of the organization and the values of the management charged with implementing the change in corporate values. All would be correct in their assessments, yet all would have missed an underlying factor of success. Despite the tenets that *competition* is good for organizational growth and success, it is my contention that too much focus is placed on competition as a positive incentive. In fact, competition is more of a disincentive and a creator of violence, instituting problems within organizations. From a violence perspective, the MBAs severed the bonds between the organization and its management teams that originally allowed the organization to be successful. Second, inclusiveness that had once been key was expunged from organizational decision making, creating an aura of mistrust and miscommunication. Third, the tenet of balancing individuality with teamwork was replaced by a unilateral decision that the corporation knows best. Fourth, the tenet of embracing new ideas and ideals was not violated directly. Instead, the organization disregarded the ideas of the profit makers—the facility managers—in favor of the standards created by the executive decision makers. This choice created imbalance within the organization. Fifth, the tenet of irresolution of power, authority, and control was violated when additional controls were instituted violating the original belief structures of the organization. The sixth tenet became the strongest factor for violence. When "the end (more profit) justifies the means (violating the outlying facility managers)" is the guiding principle, the organization creates a level of violence that management techniques cannot fix or alter. Such was the case for the Northeast Test Preparation Center.

Fiscal health and success must be balanced with adherence to organizational ideals. Successful growth and development can only be achieved when there is a balance that ensures that goals and policies mirror the actions of the corporation. Without that integrity, organizational violence becomes the normative action.

David met with many of the other facility managers of the corporation. He struggled with accepting the organizational cultural changes and wondered if it is worth it. For David, his liberal education made him want to select different options. He felt he had worked too hard in his life to now experience the violence thrust upon him. He and his wife made the move to continue to enhance their quality of life and peace of mind. The actions of the organization violated their perspective of partnership and future. Many other facility managers struggled with the same choices without reaching decisions—just trapped in the issue of violence.

The MBAs wondered what went wrong, why the loss of profit, why the reduction in sales, why the lack of new markets to pursue. They did not see their own decision making as a key to the problem, only believing that the facility managers did not know how to really be profitable. The *Washington Post* had different perspectives on the acquisition of this corporation. Were they wrong in their selection? Absolutely not. Was their change of the organizational profit structure at issue? Probably. Will they blame the facility managers, or will they look at their own actions as tantamount to the creation of violence? Not without a long revisiting of corporate decision making. Something must give.

The battle continued. The organization continued to lose part of the market share, and no real understanding of the issues occurred. David continued to evaluate his options. Remaining in the Carolinas was important; maybe remaining with the organization was not. Only time would tell; and the violence continued.

7

Southern California County Moving Through a Cultural Change: An Organizational Violence Process as an Afterthought

Marie Vasquez, a director of the Facilities Management Department of Southern California County, was distraught at the day's events. She just received a notice from the grand jury informing her that her management tactics and performance were under investigation based on complaints from employees in her department. The notice said that an investigation had begun and she would be asked to account for the actions of the management team within the department. Marie was extremely concerned because the tone of the letter suggested that the grand jury had made its decision with the employees without interviewing the management team in question and especially her.

Mike, the assistant administrative officer for Public Works and Marie's superior, heard about the notice. He recognized that not everyone agreed with Marie's management style; however, he found that the charges were inconsistent with how he perceived her management of the department. Critical to his assessment was her dedication to the department and her desire to make things right within the organization. Based on his concerns, Mike created a Request for Proposal from consultants in both management and organizational development to define strategies that could assist in the development of a realistic response to the grand jury notice. Following is the response to that Request for Proposal and the report that was originally generated.

BACKGROUND

Southern California County Facilities Management and the Administration of the Public Works Group recognized that an *organizational impasse* had developed within the Facilities Management Department. The impasse appeared to impede communication, decision making, collaboration, conflict resolution, work management, and planning throughout the department in three divisions of the organization. The impetus for the change appeared to have been initiated by a report from the Southern California County Public Employees Association to the grand jury. In the report, the association charged that Facilities Management employees were complaining significantly about low morale, reduced team effectiveness, and poor quality workmanship. They reported numerous issues affecting work within the department: low morale; increased labor-management conflict; poor record of management resolving conflicts; unsound personnel practices, including understaffed and overworked custodial personnel, undersupplied personnel, poor employee communication, nepotism and favoritism, and high turnover among clerical positions; inefficient assignment of labor, an issue raised by maintenance; poor preventive maintenance, causing buildings to deteriorate; wasting of public funds and materials; use of outside contractors; and poor safety habits and unsafe working conditions.

The management of both the Public Works Group Administration and Facilities Management determined that a structured approach to problem resolution was required to ensure a successful outcome to the identified conflicts.

Public Works and Human Resources contacted six consultants for interviews to ascertain their approach to the resolutions of the conflict. These consultants were interviewed by Facilities Management managers; Mike Davis, assistant administrative officer for Public Works; Jim Hawk, assistant administrative officer for Human Resources; and Robert Ellio and Sue Tank of the Southern California County Public Employees Association. Dr. Roger Jones, a management consultant was selected to collect the data and perform the intervention. Dr. Jones conducted interviews with the affected parties and wrote a report to Mike Davis detailing his assessment of the issues and recommending steps of action for resolution of the issues. The report submitted detailed outcomes for the department *without* discussion with the managers for a balanced assessment of the issues involved. Based on this development, Davis, in conjunction with the managers of the department, cancelled the contract with Dr. Jones. It was hoped at this time that the intervention could be accomplished with the internal organizational consultant, Nancy Taylor; however, Taylor indicated that she was unwilling to intervene as a lone consultant and stated that an additional consultant was required before she would participate in the process. At her request and with the insistence of Davis, an organizational consultant, Lloyd C. Williams, was contacted to begin the intervention process with the employees and managers of the Facilities Management Department.

The decision to utilize the services of an organizational consultant over a management consultant was significant. A *management consultant* collects data relative to given issues and directs the organization in the best approach and process based on the consultant's perspective. An *organizational consultant* recognizes the necessity to marry the beliefs and values of the employees, managers, and the system to co-create a systems change that freezes the former values, beliefs, actions, and systems of the former organization to optimize a newer culture based on changing values, beliefs, and actions for successful organizational outcomes.

It is important to note here that management of the department was not pleased with the choice of the new consultant based on their initial interview with him. Numerous interpretations (control, fear, predisposed outcomes, belief and comfort with the internal consultant) were possible causes for their reticence; however, management agreed to begin the process with the organizational consultant versus a management consultant.

Upon beginning his consultation with the Facilities Management Department, Dr. Williams was informed by Taylor that fear was rampant among the employees and managers, and trust was nonexistent. Employees feared retaliation from the managers; managers feared the process of managing, believing that any and all actions would be viewed negatively. The department was out of control.

DATA ANALYSIS AND INITIAL IMPRESSIONS

After meeting with Taylor, Dr. Williams met with the managers of the department and each of the affected employee groups: maintenance, grounds, and custodial. This session focused on allowing all employees and managers to "view" communication or the lack thereof and its resultant outcomes. Upon discussions with the employees, managers, Nancy Taylor and Mike Davis, a proposal for intervention with Facilities Management was presented to Davis, the identified client. Observations involving Facilities Management personnel indicated the following issues:

Management: Poor communication; mistrust of the employees; lack of a team environment; lack of managerial expertise; inappropriate roles within the organizational structure; lack of a systems understanding of the existing issues and their impact; and increased personalization of the dysfunctions within the department.

Employees: Poor communication; mistrust of management; lack of team orientation except in fighting management; lack of technical expertise by supervisors that affected their job roles and performance; lack of understanding of the systems and an abdication of

Figure 7.1
The Dysfunctional Communication Cycle

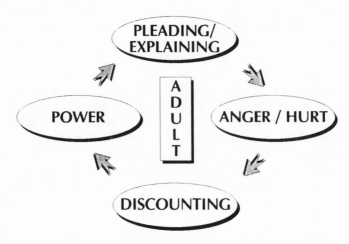

their management role; increased personalization of the dysfunctions within the department and an abdication of their responsibilities and accountabilities to ensure quality and quantity of work; and embellishment of the issues and misquoting of the facts in a consistent manner suggesting that a hidden agenda existed.

Association: Poor communication with Facilities Management managers; mistrust of management; potentially inappropriate relationship with employees, based on the lack of investigation of issues to ascertain the efficacy of the issues before formalization (this may suggest a loss of objectivity on the part of the association); lack of specifics in the letter to the grand jury, which utilized inflammatory language ("misappropriation of funds," "nepotism," "favoritism"), which could speak to the lack of objectivity; and lack of sharing complete information relating to the management of the organization, thereby contributing to a lose-lose situation.

These specific issues were manifesting themselves in a dysfunctional cycle of communication depicted in Figure 7.1, which will be explained more fully later in the chapter, under Recommendations and Discussion. In effect, management, employees, and the association appeared caught in the same trap, experiencing the same dynamics of relating to each other.

The resultant behaviors of all these dynamics from all parties involved suggested that the organization was experiencing a *systems impasse*. The systems impasse exhibits the following attributes: mistrust throughout the system; disbelief in the words, work, or actions of all involved; poor communication throughout, continually affecting any and all actions; overmanagement and extreme control by management of all actions; abdication of responsibility by maintenance supervisors; feelings of intimidation between management and employees; and retaliation and ineffective work outputs by one manager and numerous employees.

As the consultant, the first three sessions focused on systemic data collection and analysis. Instruments used for collection of data were soft data instruments based on the original data collected by Dr. Jones in his original process. The instruments for soft data collection were: Lloyd C. Williams's Six Box Theory and Belief Systems Audit (*The Congruence of People and Organizations* [Westport, CT: Quorum Books, 1993]), Jack Gibb's Trust Theory Matrix (*Trust: A New View of Personal and Organizational Development* [Los Angeles: Guild of Tutor Press, 1978]), and Kurt Weisbord's Six Box Organizational Analysis Model (*Organizational Behavior: An Applied Psychological Approach* [Dallas: Hammer and Organ, 1978]).

Soft data collection instruments were used during this intervention simultaneously with the actual intervention work to reduce the organizational and personal pain of all involved. It was apparent during the first session that the trauma and emotional pain factors were too high to subject the organization and its members to an additional battery of instruments for pure statistical purposes. Thus, to conduct the analysis separately would have been to continue the dysfunctional cycle. The results of the data collection process began to narrow down the data received to create a more accurate picture of the issues and dynamics within the Department of Facilities Management.

DATA ANALYSIS FINDINGS

During the analysis process and the initial three sessions with all participants, several findings were made. The Facilities Management Department operated from a *theological belief system* that focused on high structure, little flexibility, inhibited trust, and decision making at the highest levels of the organization. These factors inhibited the ability of the organization to effectively achieve the outcomes they define as essential to effective management and service delivery to its clients. According to Williams's Six Box Theory (see Figure 7.2), Facilities Management was dysfunctional in all six parameters within grounds, maintenance, and custodial services. *Communication* was severely structured and mistrustful. *Decision making* at the top forced all to abdicate responsibility and accountability for their actions and blame management for all decisions, good or bad. No *collaboration* occurred outside of the management group; supervisors did not talk with each other re-

Figure 7.2
The Six Box Theory

Copyright © 1987–1993 Dr. Lloyd C. Williams.

garding assignments of employees or other aspects of their role in planning, managing, or auditing the work. *Relationships* were at an all time low throughout the department. *Problem resolution* was thwarted in the department based on lack of trust, increased perceived retaliation, and poor resolution skills and techniques. Finally, little if any *understanding of the current system* occurred based on all accountability factors existing at the top of the organizational structure.

Weisbord's Six Box Model encompasses rewards, purpose and structure, helpful mechanisms, relationships, leadership, and environmental influences. According to this model, there were no clear purposes, rewards, goals, or structures identified by maintenance employees regarding the role of Facilities Management. This factor was different in the grounds and custodial sectors. Their problems did not exist in purpose, rewards, goals, or structures. Formalized issues were in relatively clear ranges of success; only process ranges were out of focus and dysfunctional.

The Public Employees Association identified all three groups as significantly dysfunctional and that morale, clear directions, and other organizational factors were out of control.

The data did not support the dysfunction but rather suggested that *process factors* were significantly out of balance throughout the organization, *not work factors*. Only maintenance was out of control and off balance in both process and work factors. There was very little trust in existence throughout the entire organization. All parties seemed to feel that the other side was "out to get them." This impeded effectiveness of work habits, supervision, work management, and budget management in the maintenance division. As trust is optimized through consistency in policies and procedures and through congruence of behavior; Facilities Management had been negligent in resolving or developing a consistent and congruent track record for developing trust among employees. Blame was being directed toward management. It was felt that Jim Franklin had significantly distorted information regarding maintenance to the director and deputy director. He also reportedly shifted his own responsibility to Ms. Vasquez, creating a feeling that she was out to get the employees or that she did not trust them. In reality, the lack of performance, planning, supervision, and management within maintenance could be attributed to Franklin himself. The director and deputy director thus instituted policies, procedures, structures, and rules to balance the issues. This process placed *all* managers in an untenable position when management of maintenance was the more appropriate target. Mismanagement of and lack of consistent work performance in the maintenance division engendered resentment from grounds and custodial. They desired resolution of maintenance's budgetary problems, and they resent doing their share of work while, they believe, maintenance does not. Franklin took a retaliatory stance towards maintenance employees because they did not respond to changes, which in turn created an escalation of the conflicts within the department. Lack of distance from management caused some maintenance employees to retaliate against management.

No real data supported the notion of nepotism within the organization. Favoritism did exist; however, it was based on utilizing employees with the most skill more often. This suggests the need for equalizing training among all the employees rather than relying on the skills of a few. These choices were made by supervisors, not management. However, management was blamed. No data existed to support the charge that Facilities Management wasted public funds. All data—management decisions reports, budget reports, and so on—suggested that management performed their functions appropriately given a consistent trend of reduction of general fund dollars and an increased requirement to make up budgetary needs through reimbursable costs. At the time of the analysis, maintenance poorly managed its budget, thereby creating shortages. Better fiscal management of maintenance was required to ensure that employees and supervisors can more effectively plan the work to be performed so that all reimbursable dollars can be realized and to ensure the success of the division in meeting its goals.

Policies from the Board of County Supervisors, albeit appropriate, were not consistent with all organizational needs. Outside contractors were used when utilization of existing staff was impossible or infeasible. The existence of fewer general fund dollars supported the idea that understaffing occurred. Better planning and potential restructuring could allow successful accomplishment of the work without a significant increase in staff. Personnel practices were the responsibility of Human Resources. Where advancement did not occur for some employees, the blame for this was shared. Facilities Management did not train where required, and employees did not take responsibility for upgrading their own skills. Thus, blaming only management was inappropriate. Employees were not undersupplied; rather, better management of and inventory control at the warehouse was required. A dispatcher position would significantly assist the organization in more effectively accomplishing the work scope of the maintenance division. The creation of the position was the responsibility of the maintenance and construction superintendent Franklin, not the director and deputy director. Some positions within the "general maintenance worker" classification should be upgraded to "general maintenance mechanic." The fact that no oversight of out-of-class work was being performed within maintenance contributed to the increased resentment within the division. Unfortunately, this responsibility also belonged to the Franklin, not the director and deputy director.

Because the issues of the grounds, custodial, and maintenance divisions were all different, resolution of the issues needed to be different. Specifically, what was designed for maintenance may not have been appropriate for either of the other areas and vice versa.

According to the Grand Jury report, the clerical staff on the whole felt sufficiently managed and treated fairly by the organization and perceived no need for intervention at this time or in the past. Employees who previously stated concerns were no longer with the organization, they either retired or were transferred. Numerous problems existed for a few employees; a few problems existed for most of the employees; and a number of employees had no complaints at all. However, the "vocal minority" were cast as the "silent majority," thereby allowing their views to be perceived as those of the majority when that was not the case. At issue was the need for importance, power, and control. Unfortunately, it appears as though the Public Employees Association believed the few and did not necessarily assess the majority, thereby distorting the magnitude of the issues.

These findings are discussed more comprehensively in the next section of this chapter. Recommendations are made for actions by the department. These recommendations encompass multiple findings in a systematic fashion so that management and employees can develop a planned approach to changes within the department. Additionally, this chapter is structured so that the reader can understand the process involved in creating each recommendation.

THEORETICAL PERSPECTIVE FOR THE CONSULTATION

Historical Background

The intervention with Facilities Management was conducted utilizing the Belief Systems/Congruence Model developed by Dr. Williams. The model is predicated on the premise that people's values change based on new information and ideas, but beliefs and the concept of belief systems as baseline frameworks for people and system rarely change. From this perspective, the Facilities Management organization—the managers and the employees—all operate from a given belief system.

There are three belief systems that affect personal and organizational functioning. I have titled the belief systems based on their historical underpinnings.

THEOLOGICAL BELIEF SYSTEM: The theological belief system focuses on the ability of people and organizational systems to be comfortable with society and rules as they currently exist. Knowledge and rules that impede chaos in one's life or in an organization are of extreme importance. The value set, therefore, that governs this belief system is the *work value set*. The work value set views getting the work accomplished as the highest and governing need. Creativity and helping others feel comfortable are of secondmost importance. Understanding the system (how the organization is structured and operates) is of third importance. Of least importance is feelings of self and others. Empowerment has no place in this system. The goal is to have society and systems comply with the rules and procedures.

LEGAL BELIEF SYSTEM: The legal belief system is an outgrowth of the Theist process and focuses on the attainment and maintenance of power, authority, and control in the hands of a few. People and organizational systems see the value of history and maintaining things as they currently are as the most important outcome. Therefore, the value set that governs is the *communal value set*. Maintaining the view and operations of the whole is of the highest importance. Getting things accomplished is of secondary importance. Understanding the history and systems is of third importance; and how you and others feel is of last importance.

PSYCHOLOGICAL BELIEF SYSTEM: The psychological belief system is an anathema to the other two belief systems. Where the other two belief systems place importance and prominence on control, rules, power, and authority this belief system looks at the uniqueness of the individual or the system and the importance of the group from a proactive rather than a reactive stance. Empowerment and personal control to make choices and participate freely are desired goals. Therefore, the two value sets *we orientation* and *individuation* govern the psychological belief system. Both value sets are synonymous, but one speaks to the individual and the other to the group. Determining who you are, who the group is, and how you feel is the highest need of this belief system. Understanding the system's operation is of secondmost importance, for knowledge of the surroundings and operations lends credence to empowerment. Being creative and innovative is the third need, as it supports movement outside one's comfort zones in order to be effective. Getting the actual job done is the last component, for there is no need to act and perform without understanding all the issues.

The Process

From the beginning of this intervention, it was apparent that the managers and employees of Facilities Management were working toward different goals. This was understandable because the employees, the managers, and the system were all operating from different belief systems. The organization itself was using the theological belief system. One manager was using a combination theological/legal belief system, while two other managers were using a combination theological/psychological belief system. The employees were using a combination psychological/legal belief system.

These differences were the underlying factors contributing to the dysfunction within the department. Managers believed that the system of rules and the organizational structure were fair and valid, that decisions should be made at the top, and that tight control on the activities of the employees was necessary and acceptable to do the job well. Employees, on the other hand, believed that they should be able to control a large component of their job and that authority and control should be shared. These differing perspectives set the stage for the arguments, miscommunication, and underlying mistrust among the departmental staff.

The objective of this intervention was to assist all sides in making significant fundamental shifts in the way they perceive each other and the system. Specifically, managers needed to realize that their view of the organization was contributing to the pain and trauma the employees were experiencing. Each time management made a decision for the employees without including the employees in the decision-making process, they contributed to the employees' dissatisfaction and mistrust.

Each time the employees complained or disagreed with management, management felt betrayed and abused by the employees. As management felt threatened, they moved from the theological belief system to their secondary stance, the legal belief system. They wanted to get more control over the situation so that life could become more relaxed and chaos-free. As management shifted to a legal belief system, so did the employees. The employees stated that empowerment was critical for them; however, every time control was exerted by management, employees exerted their power and control by slowing down work, making multiple trips to accomplish one job, and soliciting Public Workers letters from the Association. There was and is a continuing need for management and employees to maintain an open communication process to ensure that the dysfunctions do not reoccur in the future.

This process went on for two years. Because of the length of time, both management and employees were locked into their legal belief systems, under stress and duress.

The consultant faced some questions. Can management and the employees back away from their belief systems long enough to look at the issues creating their joint dysfunctions? If not, can management and the employees develop tools that free them from their pain long enough to create one common belief system for operating within the Facilities Management Department?

The consultant determined that creating tools was essential to free all participants from their pain long enough to create a new, shared belief system. This meant that Facilities Management needed to experience a *systems change*. This dynamic process was initially presented to the managers and the assistant administrative officer for Public Works during a retreat. The managers felt comfortable with the process and were able to "loosen the reins" to allow movement to occur within the organizational environment. The harder task was getting the employees to look at their own dynamics and stop blaming management for all the ills of the department. Most of the employees understood their own part in the dysfunction, but a vocal minority of six employees refused to look at their role in the dysfunction because operating from their legal belief system gave them lots of power. They enjoyed that power and chose to maintain it through complaints, through stating that "nothing has changed," and through repeated misinformation to the association assuming that their views were the views of all department employees.

The techniques used throughout the intervention in the six recommendations discussed below were designed to move the organization from differing belief systems to one belief system: a *legal/psychological belief system*, stressing the critical necessity to be flexible, not rigid. This shift would allow all participants to win, as was the case at the start of the intervention.

RECOMMENDATIONS AND DISCUSSION

Recommendation #1

> That Facilities Management participate in an ongoing process of com-
> munication to enhance the levels of trust, collaboration, and consistency
> while simultaneously utilizing the communication process as an avenue
> of problem resolution.

From the point of intervention, it became clear that movement toward
change and resolution of issues would not be possible without a significant enhancement of trust and communication. Based on this assumption and premise (supported by substantial documentation), a
process of intervention was begun with all three Facilities Management
groups—management, employees, and the association.

The first component of the intervention was to alter the process and
style of communication within the entire department. The Facilities Management Department operated from a dysfunctional communication
cycle (see figure 7.1). The cycle is predicated on the escalating evolutional
principle that moves individuals away from clear and direct adult communication to a process of pleading. The pleading process focuses on
the inability of people to own up to what has occurred around them.
Rather than own one's behavior, actions, and thoughts, the start of
communication is characterized by making excuses or blaming others.
The first response of the listener is to either discount the communication
given or become angered or hurt by the communication. The reaction
(an activity against something or someone) causes the initiator to become
angry or to discount in return. When anger or discounting does not get
the response desired, then the use of power becomes the next step. In
the case of Facilities Management, the pleading process initiated the
dysfunctional communication cycle; employees or managers made excuses, spoke for sympathy, or defended their actions in the communication process. Anger was the reaction to the pleading; behaviors would
become either explosive, silent, or manipulative. If the ego of the listening party was not strong, discounting would be the avenue of choice,
where the behaviors were avoidance, silence, or belittlement. When
these tactics did not achieve the desired results, power became the next
step. Employees would invoke the name of the association or the grand
jury; managers would invoke authority or the name of the director. In
each case, defiance, offensive behavior, belittlement, and manipulation
became the tools of the power process in the communication cycle.
Figure 7.3 includes these details. All components were inappropriate
and ineffective in establishing good communication among all parties.

The employees and managers of Facilities Management found them-

Figure 7.3
The Dysfunctional Communication Cycle Extended

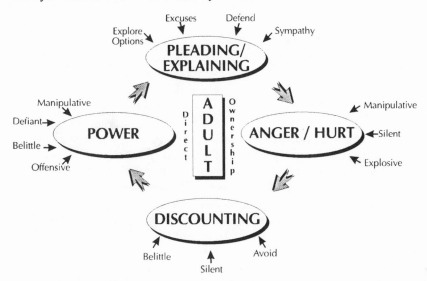

selves permanently mired in this dysfunctional parameter. Communication became a process of protecting oneself from the attacks and belittlement of others. The dysfunction made objective, open-minded listening impossible, even if the information being shared was accurate and essential for change, quality performance, increased production, or enhancement of work planning. Mistrust was rampant.

The consultant team determined that it would be more helpful if the managers and employees could learn to alter their communication in such a fashion that defeating the other was not a criterion for the communication; rather, that equal sharing and achieving a win/win situation would be the goal. The consultants, therefore, spent time allowing managers and employees to communicate with and confront each other on their pains, failures, and successes, while pointing out where communication was effective and where prior unresolved conflict was impeding their ability to listen to the other party. The process was a long and arduous one, wrought with significant past emotional events guiding current behavior and that triggering reactions rather than responses that encourage effective communication.

Managers and employees significantly increased their communication patterns. Their ability to "hear one another" improved to the extent that they were able to create strategies for change, alter structures for enhanced work performance, and confront each other where they believe conflicts and unfair labeling was occurring. The improved communi-

cation guided their abilities to co-create recommendations for more effective functioning within the work environment.

Recommendation #2

That Facilities Management enhance the performance of the department employees by altering the working style and relationships within
the department to create a more accountable and responsible system
for accomplishing the work at the lowest level of the organization.

In the communication process, employees felt that they were not
treated as adults, capable of providing quality work performance. The
consultants worked with the employee teams and managers to co-create
an accountability responsibility system. This system was created to allow
managers and employees to structurally and mentally assess where personal and professional boundaries were being violated. To achieve this,
the employees and managers were taught the Williams Six Box Theory
shown in Figure 7.2. This theory states that all persons operate from a
system that works effectively as long as each individual is not confronted
by any other system. When two systems meet, the possibility for conflict
arises. To ensure effectiveness of each system, people need to understand the components and parameters of that system.

The Six Box Theory introduced to the organization focuses on allowing
each person to categorize all actions and thoughts in six areas: communication, decision making, problem resolution, relationship building,
collaboration, and system understanding. These areas help create a "full
understanding" of any issue—work scope, policies, peers, management,
family, personal or organizational perspective, values, or beliefs. For
every issue, one must assess how well the information has been communicated; whether relationships exist and how to build on those relationships to improve performance; the work to be performed, including
what skills are required, how the work is communicated, and who needs
to collaborate with another to accomplish the tasks; how to resolve problems that arise and how to explore options before making decisions
regarding actions to be taken.

Each level of an organization (management/supervisors/employees) is
limited in the scope of responsibilities that fall within its level of accountability. Management is accountable for policy development; employees are not. Managers are not accountable for performing the work
of the organization; employees are. Supervisors plan the overall job at
their level of accountability; employees determine how that planned
work will be accomplished. Where accountability factors are different at
each organizational level, all levels must work together to achieve success in the work and in the workplace (see Figure 7.4).

Figure 7.4
Whose Job Is It? Quantity and Quality of Work

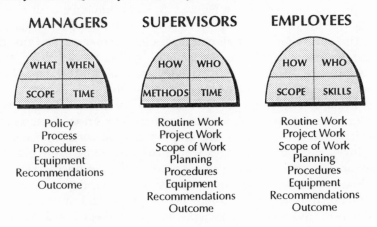

MANAGERS	SUPERVISORS	EMPLOYEES
WHAT WHEN	HOW WHO	HOW WHO
SCOPE TIME	METHODS TIME	SCOPE SKILLS

Policy	Routine Work	Routine Work
Process	Project Work	Project Work
Procedures	Scope of Work	Scope of Work
Equipment	Planning	Planning
Recommendations	Procedures	Procedures
Outcome	Equipment	Equipment
	Recommendations	Recommendations
	Outcome	Outcome

VIA

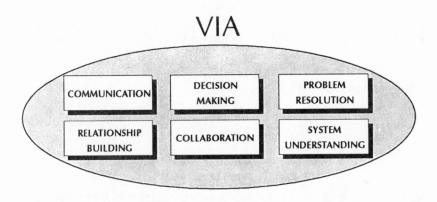

COMMUNICATION	DECISION MAKING	PROBLEM RESOLUTION
RELATIONSHIP BUILDING	COLLABORATION	SYSTEM UNDERSTANDING

The process to reach this objective was instituted after a meeting with all employees. The employees also participated in the development and creation of a change in the structure of the maintenance division. The concerns raised by the employees involved broadening the assignments given to perform the full range of their trade within the confines of the scopes of work belonging to the department. Management's concern in the process was receiving assurances from the employees and supervisors that work scope levels would be maintained, budgets monitored, supervision improved, and accountability levels monitored. The employees diligently worked with the supervisors to create a structure that maintained the following: better utilization of staff, increased skill enhancement of employees, more potential to perform requisition work, better utilization of the estimator and scheduler, a reporting relationship to one supervisor, more accountability for all employees, checks and balances with accounting for all job costs, and a rotational spray booth.

This process, as depicted in Figure 7.5, went into effect four months after the meeting with the employees, with the full support of management. The critical factor for all employees and managers was ensuring that they maintain a level of performance that addressed these issues in an appropriate manner, and that they maintain the Six Box Theory to avoid reverting back to old styles of performing.

It is important to recognize that all changes that were made were transitional in nature. Facilities Management was an evolving organization. Therefore, it would be presumptuous for anyone to believe that the changes were final. Changes would continue to be made based on performance criteria; changing strategic issues like contract services versus inhouse services; or changing needs within the department, such as a downturn in service requirements for carpenters or an upturn of maintenance mechanics and general service workers based on carpet requisition work. The critical factor was the ability of the organization, its management, and its employees, to "read the changing tides" and adjust the organizational structure to meet the needs of the mission while continually enhancing the human potential of the organization.

Recommendation #3

> That Facilities Management begin the process of upgrading the skills of management and supervisors through a training program and individualized coaching for the maintenance and construction superintendent.

One of the findings in the data analysis was the lack of critical managerial skills on the part of the maintenance supervisors and the necessity to upgrade the skills of all other supervisors and managers. Numerous reports from the employees and managers suggested that supervisors were in many ways abdicating their responsibility and accountability to manage the work and lead the employees through planning, coaching, and responsible leadership. Supervisors stated that they had no authority or control; however, they did not live up to their own responsibility to take action. These factors were different in the grounds and custodial divisions. Supervisors in these two areas seemed ready to assume responsibility for their work scope. Maintenance supervisors constantly reported that accountability and responsibility were not given to them by the maintenance and construction superintendent. Maintenance supervisors acted as though they had never supervised but that they functioned more as lead employees. This, therefore, short-circuited

Figure 7.5
Proposed Organizational Change for the Maintenance Division

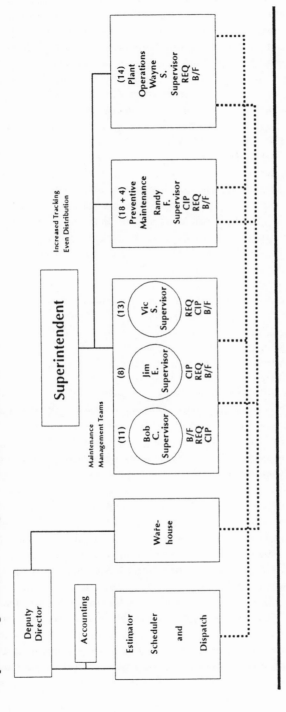

Projected Outcomes:

1) Better Utilization of Staff
2) Increased Skill Enhancement of Employees
3) More Potential to Perform Requisition Work
4) Better Utilization of Estimator and Scheduler
5) Maintain Reporting to One Supervisor
6) More Accountability for All Employees
7) Checks and Balances with Accounting for All Job Costs
8) Rotational Spray Booth

management's ability to effectively get the work accomplished in the maintenance environment.

The first requirement was to alter how supervisors and employees perceived their roles. The work could only be accomplished through a team approach; therefore, changes needed to move toward developing a win/win perspective regarding work and supervision. Training and group dynamics sessions were held to move all employees and supervisors from the lose/lose position of power, authority, and control to the win/win position of change, collaboration, and empowerment. This was a difficult process for maintenance supervisors because it required them to accept ownership for their actions. Going back to the dysfunctional communication cycle (Figure 7.1), maintenance supervisors were required to give up their pleading and become adults in the supervisory process. The developmental process of "becoming" was difficult for each. They had to begin to display courage and become more direct and clear in their responses to employees and managers.

As for the managers—the director, deputy director, and maintenance and construction superintendent—movement toward a win/win situation meant allowing failures to occur. This was extremely difficult for them because they were used to accepting responsibility and accountability for work products and actions that did not belong to them. They began to recognize that their actions, codependent in nature, perpetuated the lose/lose process, depicted in Figure 7.6.

From a belief systems perspective, management and the employees wanted to alter significantly the theological belief system of the department. This system focuses on the ability of people and organizations to be comfortable with society and rules as they currently exist. Knowledge and rules that prevent chaos are of extreme importance. The work value ethic is therefore the governing parameter—we are valued by what we do and produce. Being creative is of secondary importance, understanding the system is tertiary, and empowerment is of last or of no importance. The difficulty with Facilities Management utilizing this belief system was their inability to accomplish work because all decision making, communication, systems understanding, relationship building, and collaboration occurred only at the top level of the organization. This unknowingly was defeating their desired goals and outcomes.

To be successful, a balanced systemic approach was required. This means that management had to alter its perspective about employees' ability to perform and become empowered to be successful. This would free management to perform its own roles and become equally successful.

Recognizing this requirement for change, managers and employees devised a results-oriented belief system that valued empowerment, collaboration, participation/teamwork, and hope/trust shown in Table 7.1.

Figure 7.6
Lose/Lose, Win/Win Process

Win/Win

**Clarity
Courage
Directness**

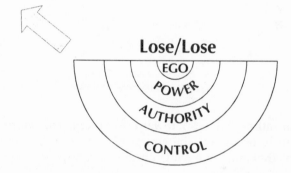

Lose/Lose

They determined the changes they desired and the outcomes they expected to achieve, and acted on them.

One additional component was required in altering behavior on the part of managers, supervisors, and employees prior to training all supervisors in upgrading their skills. All members of the organization were ineffectual in respectfully responding to issues of resistance. Therefore, training was provided to all in the area of resistance management, explained in Figure 7.7. This was very important. Throughout the data analysis process, the consultant was often struck by the amount of pseudoresistance existing among the employees. Employees often were able only to express feelings rather than to provide specific behavior to act on those feelings validating authentic resistance. Their purpose was to

Table 7.1
Results-Oriented Belief System

BELIEF SYSTEM VALUES	CHANGES DESIRED	OUTCOMES
Empowerment	1) More accountability, authority for Supervisor to design work scope. Hire Super. for Inmate program.	Empowerment Collaboration Trust Change
Collaboration	2) Supervisors should have shared accountability for budgeting & budget management.	Collaboration Empowerment Teamwork
Participation / Teamwork	3) Create flexibility for workday: 4, 10, & 50 hours.	Change Hope Empowerment
Hope / Trust	4) Negotiating w/HR to increase Internal Promotions.	Participation Empowerment Change
	5) Revisit policies, clarify.	Change Collaboration Trust
	6) Be own internal inventory system. Work budget to meet needs.	Change Empowerment Trust

create fear rather than work toward resolution. The interesting dynamic that began to occur was the empowerment of employees to challenge the complaints and statements of other employees around the authenticity of the complaint.

Employees and managers learned to honor resistance, bring it to the surface, and explore it rather than break it down, avoid it, or invoke history in terms of how things were in the past.

Major Trainings

With these initials factors having been addressed, it was now time to consider skill training for the supervisors throughout the department. As the number of supervisors was more than twenty, it was felt that a program should be developed to begin the process of training and staff development. The consulting firm designed such a training program entitled, "Steps for Creating Excellence Through Effective Supervision," illustrated in Figure 7.8. The training program was divided into four primary sections: baseline skills, management skills, critical skills, and supervision skills: The training established a framework for all supervisors and managers for leading employees and managing the work.

Figure 7.7
Resistance Management

Current Style

Break It Down:	Threaten, Coerce, Sell, Reason.
Avoid It:	Deny, Discount, Induce Guilt.
Invoke History:	Tradition, Rules, Policies.

Proposed Style

Positive Resistance

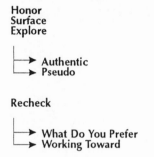

Honor
Surface
Explore

→ Authentic
→ Pseudo

Recheck

→ What Do You Prefer
→ Working Toward

Special Sessions for the Maintenance and Construction
Superintendent

Eight coaching sessions were provided for Franklin, the maintenance and construction superintendent, to enhance his skills in resolving conflicts, leading his staff, managing their work, and upgrading his interpersonal skills. The consultant saw a self-righteous component to Franklin's belief that the employees were wrong, bad, or unreliable and therefore needed to be watched, monitored, and followed. This process of investigation made it very difficult for any employee under his management to believe that change would ever occur within the department. Helping Franklin alter his demeanor, body posture, gruff language, and perspective was difficult. One statement or action of an employee could start the chain reaction for a "downward spiral" in the relationship-building or supervisory process. The interesting dynamic in this process was the ability of the superintendent to perform the functions admirably in the presence of the consultant, but he would continue to dysfunctionally lead and manage when the consultant was not present. Specifically, the employees and maintenance supervisors still felt unable to

Figure 7.8
Staff Development Programs

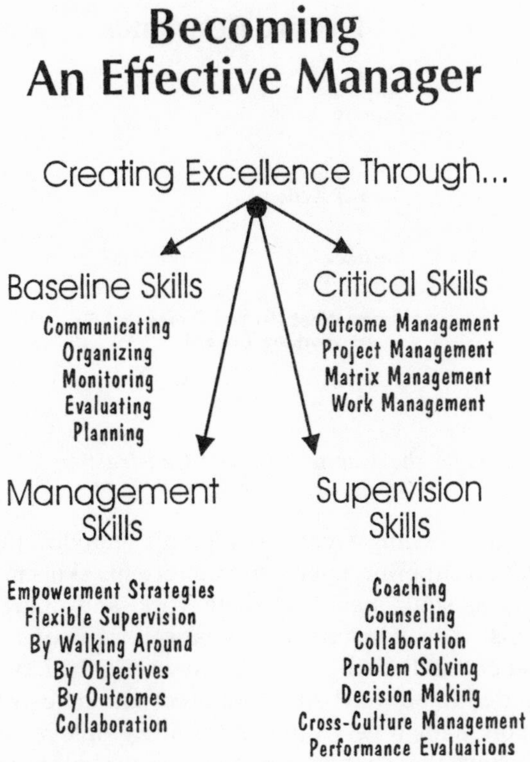

Becoming
An Effective Manager

Creating Excellence Through...

Baseline Skills

Communicating
Organizing
Monitoring
Evaluating
Planning

Critical Skills

Outcome Management
Project Management
Matrix Management
Work Management

Management Skills

Empowerment Strategies
Flexible Supervision
By Walking Around
By Objectives
By Outcomes
Collaboration

Supervision Skills

Coaching
Counseling
Collaboration
Problem Solving
Decision Making
Cross-Culture Management
Performance Evaluations

lead or manage based on directions or instructions provided them by the superintendent. It is, therefore, not clear whether or not Franklin can manage effectively; rather, the issue is whether or not his self-righteous beliefs impede his ability to manage in a successful manner.

To assist with this factor and other issues of the Six Box Theory, a weekend session with all department managers and the assistant administrative officer of Public Works was considered.

Recommendation #4

That Facilities Management develop a weekend training event for the managers of the department to more effectively create a team environment to embrace organizational change.

It had become apparent that a more effective team environment among the managers was essential to the overall organizational success of the intervention. As the consultant, a weekend event was planned for the managers.

The managers of the department felt significantly bruised by all the issues and accusations identified by the employees and the Public Employees Association. As most persons do when attacked, the managers had become entrenched in maintaining their stance of accuracy and control. Change was only going to occur if wounds could be healed. This meant that new skills needed to be learned regarding communication, power, influence, beliefs and breaking the cycle of pain. Without these new skills, healing and communication would not occur, and change would be impossible.

Primary in this process was allowing the managers to vent their pain. This meant expressing their anger, hurt, sorrow, and feelings that they were treated unfairly. They believed that the organization in general, Southern California County, and the grand jury had judged them and that they were not being given an equal opportunity to share their side of the issues. In many ways, this perspective was true, as evidenced by the behavior of the organization. Specifically, a new grand jury had been seated and intruded into the process, adding fuel to the fire. The new grand jury allowed employees and the association to work and express themselves *outside of the agreed upon process*. The grand jury subcommittee intruded into meetings without warning the department, the assistant administrative officer, or the consultant, which was perceived as a deliberate attempt by the managers to embarrass or discipline. In effect, the result was a theatrical display by maintenance employees for the benefit of the grand jury that was diametrically opposite of their behavior outside the presence of the grand jury. Comments made to Marie Vasquez by the subcommittee chair of the grand jury, such as "Marie An-

Figure 7.9
Problem-Solving Steps

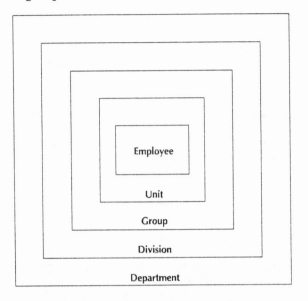

1. Identify the Problem and the Feeling with That Problem.
2. Generate Alternatives.
3. Evaluate Alternatives and Select One That All Agree to.
4. Establish Plan for Change and Time Frame for Evaluation.
5. Implement.
6. Evaluate.
7. Go Back to Number One and Rework or Fine-Tune.

toinette lost her head, you know," continued to support management's belief that the organization had already made up its mind.

Therefore, time was spent empowering the managers to change and influence their own lives rather than abdicating their power to others. Managers addressed how to create win/win situations within the department, how to empower the employees, how to co-manage their communication to enhance the building of relationships with the employees, and how to effectively create change. They addressed how to manage resistance and frustration, and they learned a model for problem resolution, depicted in Figure 7.9.

This weekend session also allowed a more effective working relationship to develop between the department and the assistant administrative officer's unit within the Public Works group.

Management felt positive upon the completion of the weekend, energized to respond more effectively with the employees, and empowered to let go of control and allow all divisions of the department to manage themselves. The weekend sessions provided the information necessary for management to perform its role well within the larger organizational environment.

Recommendation #5

That Facilities Management create an organizational structure that empowers staff, requires teamwork and collaboration, and establishes accountability and responsibility at the lowest levels of the organization.

Throughout the organizational development intervention, the focus was on the creation of a more effective working relationship between management and employees. This was achieved through the training of most employees in more effective communication skills, enhanced decision-making strategies, improved problem resolution skills, collaborative models for working together, and a better understanding of the systems operation within Facilities Management. Employees and management embraced the movement to Williams's Six Box Theory (Figure 7.3) for effective roles and systems interaction. Engaging this system allowed the members of the organization simultaneously to focus on their personal and organizational development in responding to human, managerial, and executive issues and to focus on their appropriate work roles for the future.

A component of this process caused the employees to alter their work to better meet their personal needs while maximizing the mission of the department. Each division (grounds, custodial, and maintenance) examined its current structure and created a new structure that allowed for growth and development while ensuring accountability for quality and quantity of work at the lowest level of the organization. The largest change was in the maintenance division. Based on all the changes, a flattened organizational structure was created to aid in the implementation of the goals of personal and organizational empowerment, collaboration, enhanced communication, accountability, and decision making at the lowest level of the organization.

The essence of the structural change involved the reassignment of the existing classification of maintenance and construction superintendent from the Facilities Management Department (see Figure 7.10) This reassignment of the position and the incumbent allowed the Facilities Management Department to flatten and empower the organization in a

Figure 7.10
Current Organizational Structure

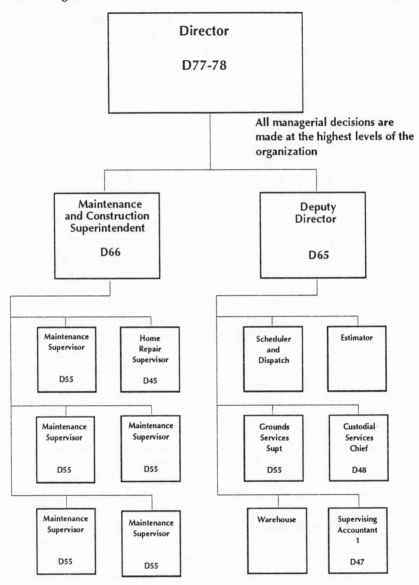

Tiered Structure
Top-Down Decision Making
Accountability at Top Levels of Organization
Singular Function Roles
Directors control Policy and Process

nontiered structure that placed accountability and responsibility on each employee and manager in a more comprehensive manner than in the past. The void created within the department would be addressed by the creation of a building services superintendent. This position's scope was somewhat different than that of the maintenance and construction superintendent. The role of the maintenance and construction superintendent was to manage only the maintenance function of the Facilities Management Department. The role of building services superintendent involved planning all the work of maintenance, collaborating with the scheduler and the estimator to ensure the creation of effective job standards and to accurately schedule all jobs performed by the maintenance division, interfacing with the regulatory compliance coordinator of the Public Works Administration Group, managing the performance of all staff involved in the maintenance division, and collaborating with the deputy director and director of Facilities Management in the development, administration, and evaluation of the budget affecting the maintenance division.

Additionally, a new position of administrative services manager would be created within the Facilities Management Department, indicated in the proposed structure in Figure 7.11. This position would replace that of the supervising accountant. No job loss would occur because the incumbent supervising accountant would become the administrative services manager. This new classification would be accountable for managing the accounting staff, the estimator, the scheduler, the warehouse staff, and the home repair division. The home repair division was included because of the unique funding issues associated with the division, and the estimator and scheduler would be utilized to more effectively accomplish the work of that division. This allowed for a more even flow of inventory control, fiscal development and management for the entire department, and tracking of overall project job performance and job cost accounting.

It was proposed that both positions, building services superintendent and administrative services manager, be classified at the D-63 level, consistent with the duties and responsibilities of this type of employee. It was also felt that to be consistent throughout the department, two additional classifications needed to be evaluated for changes in pay rate. The custodial services chief and the deputy director appeared to be misaligned based on responsibilities.

The custodial services chief was classified as a D-48; however, his responsibilities involved managing a division of seventy-four employees in all facets of managerial operations. The responsibilities were consistent with those of the grounds services superintendent classified as a D-55. It seemed appropriate to create consistency between these two like-minded positions by classifying the custodial services chief as a D-55 as well (Figure 7.11 reflects these changes).

The deputy director role under the proposed changes would be ac-

Figure 7.11
Proposed Organizational Structure

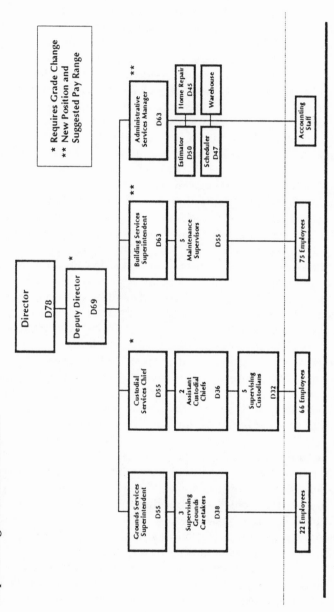

* Requires Grade Change
** New Position and
Suggested Pay Range

Director
D78

Deputy Director *
D69

Grounds Services
Superintendent
D55

Supervising 3
Grounds
Caretakers
D38

22 Employees

Custodial Services Chief *
D55

Assistant 2
Custodial
Chiefs
D36

Supervising 5
Custodians
D32

66 Employees

Building Services **
Superintendent
D63

Maintenance 5
Supervisors
D55

75 Employees

Administrative **
Services Manager
D63

Estimator
D50

Home Repair
D45

Scheduler
D47

Warehouse

Accounting
Staff

Flatten Organizational Structure
Shared Decision Making
Accountability at the Lowest Levels
of the Organization

Dual Functional Roles
Team Response in Policy and Process
Quality and Quantity Focused

Table 7.2
Fiscal Year 1991–1992 Impact

Grade/Salary Data	Deputy Director	Administrative Svcs. Mgr.	Building Svcs. Superintendent	Custodial Services Chief	Net Change
Current Grade/Salary *	D65/E $25.43	D54/A $15.98	D66/E $26.07	D48/E $16.80	
New Grade/Salary *	D69/D $26.72	D63/A $19.91	D63/A $19.91	D55/2 $17.63	
Difference	$1.29	$3.92	($6.17)	$0.83	
Increased Cost for FY 1991/92 with change commencing PP 5 (2/8/92)	$1,031.68	$3,136.64	($4,933.76)	$665.60	($99.84)

* Including 4% salary increase effective 1/1/92

countable for the maintenance division, encompassing eighty additional employees and differing scopes of work not currently maintained in the classification. It was therefore felt that no title change was required, but a change to a pay rate of D-69 was required, based on the added responsibilities.

Fiscal Impact of Proposed Organizational Changes

On the surface, it might appear that the fiscal impact of such changes was substantial. Upon charting the changes (see Table 7.2), taking into consideration 4 percent increases in January 1992 and July 1992, it is evident that the changes were not significant. From February 1, 1992, to June 30, 1992, Facilities Management realized a total savings of $99.84. For the next fiscal year, additional costs for the changes amounted to $6,107.95, as shown in Table 7.3. It was believed that these proposed changes would significantly enhance the performance future of the Facilities Management Department. These changes were discussed with the director and deputy director of Facilities Management and the assistant administrative officer of Public Works and met with favor for enhancing the overall performance of the department.

The recommendations suggested that a systems change was occurring within the department. The executive management had seriously and in good faith assessed its responsibility to Public Works, the employees of Facilities Management, and Southern California County as a governmental entity. This partial response spoke to that commitment and dedication. Performance enhancement, collaboration, increased com-

Table 7.3
Fiscal Year 1992–1993 Impact

Current Grade/Salary *	D65/E $26.45	D54/B $17.47	D66/E $27.12	D48 $17.46	
New Grade/Salary *	D69/D $27.79 for 3 PP	D63/A $20.71 for 3 PP	D66/A $20.71 for 3 PP	D55/2 $18.33 for 3 PP	
	D69/E $29.18 for 23 PP	D63/B $21.75 for 23 PP	D66/B $21.75 for 23 PP	D55/3 $19.26 for 23 PP	
Difference	$5,354.95	$8,652.40	($11,419.60)	$3,520.20	($6,107.95)

* Including 4% salary increase effective 7/1/92

munication, improved decision making, and clearer delineation and understanding of the system are all components of creating an effective managerial and employee system.

It was, therefore, hoped that the administration of Southern California County would implement these proposed changes and direct the various departments required to sign the changes to continue to assist Facilities Management in its endeavors to enhance and improve the department and its employees.

Recommendation #6

That Facilities Management enhance the relationship between the Public Employees Association and management through the implementation of a one-day workshop on problem resolution and collaboration.

In the original proposal, a three-day workshop with the association was proposed for problem resolution and collaboration. Throughout the intervention process, the consultant purposefully excluded the association from the intervention. This was done under the belief that change within the department was the desired outcome of the association. It was later discovered in discussions with the association that change within the department was critical but that, inclusion in the process was an additional outcome.

The consultant spent three sessions with the association leadership to start the process of "healing their wounds" resulting from being excluded. It was important to the consultant that blame be placed on him rather than on the department. Upon establishing that fact, discussing communication parameters, and negotiating desired outcomes for a one-day workshop, a program for change was designed. The workshop was entitled "Interagency Collaboration: Moving on a Continuum Toward the 'Win/Win.' "

The workshop focused on conflict resolution, interagency collaboration and effective communication, and creative strategies for outcomes development. Management and the association had matching outcomes for the session: better communication, increased trust, and a less formalized process to deal with all issues. They looked at teamwork, commitment, perseverance, consistency, and credibility as avenues for change and interagency collaboration. Critical in the process was the ability to differ without getting angry, discounting the content of the other party, or utilizing power. The collaboration process instead focused on the ability of both parties to win.

Management and the association agreed to: make commitments to change the current cycle of working together, practice the changes, be open to challenges from the other, operate from trust rather than mistrust and deceit, accept responsibility for leading the change, confront the truth about their behaviors and policies, be consistent, be congruent in actions and words, be open and nonjudgmental, and identify outcomes jointly.

The association and management of Facilities Management genuinely appeared dedicated to developing a working relationship that would meet the needs of their special interests. Only time would tell whether or not a working relationship would truly be developed.

A new association representative, Jim Weik, assumed the responsibilities for this department. To that end, a working relationship was established. Weik would continue to initiate all requests relative to the department to the deputy director. Prior to any formal grievances, the two parties would sit and discuss the options and potential parameters of resolution. Where possible, as many issues as possible would be resolved outside of the formal process; in any case, trust would be the basis for discussion rather than mistrust. Elliot, the labor representative, and the deputy director, Davis, agreed to meet on a monthly basis to assess the working relationship between the department and the association. This would help resolve issues that affected procedure, process, or policy.

The working relationship between the association and the department appeared to improve. Continued movement toward collaboration was required for long-range success in this area.

ISSUES LIST

Resolution of Specific Problems Addressed During the Consultation

During the course of the consultation, numerous issues surfaced that got in the way of overall systems change. Following are an explanation of these issues and the resolutions agreed upon during the consultation.

Retaliation

Employees felt that retaliation was a central concern. To create a decrease in this behavior, clear guidelines were created for reporting relationships that distanced the maintenance and construction superintendent from the employees. This significantly aided in building trust among the employees and the confidence level of the supervisors of the maintenance division. This was not an issue for grounds or custodial.

Departmental Morale

An organizational change was created to allow more empowerment, accountability, and responsibility for each employee. This process significantly aided in boosting the morale of the employees, helping them believe that "real change was possible through this process. Employees were able to determine their own lunch breaks, purchase supplies with the approval of the supervisors, restructure their work based on their perspective of the most effective way to perform the work, and plan their work according to their own judgment. This lifted morale considerably.

Poor Record of Management Resolving Conflicts

By using the Six Box Theory, management and employees began to establish clear limits and parameters for their functioning. This enabled everyone to be clear about where the lines of accountability rested, and it created a system for problem resolution throughout the department. In effect, employees and managers actively assessed whether the problems were occurring in the areas of communication, decision making, collaboration, or problem solving or a misunderstanding of the operations of the system.

Maintenance Employee Work Assignments

With the advent of supervisors taking more responsibility, a new process for work assignment came into force. Employees were given series of work to perform where they were accountable for how that work was completed. This allowed more discussion and negotiation between employees and their supervisors on the work assignments. Additionally, employees within maintenance redesigned the structure of maintenance to encourage more effective accomplishment of work and performance of the full scope of their classification. The restructuring was done in conjunction with the supervisors, including management buy-in, thereby reducing friction. In grounds, the rotational work assignments began, and eighteen-month rotations were initiated to equalize the skills of inside and outside crews and to more even distribute the work. Painters in maintenance also created a rotational process. There were very few issues within grounds; however, supervisors' skills were enhanced, and communication and problem resolution skills were improved. In custodial, the employees focused on work assignments and understaffing. Through discussion, issues of miscommunication surrounding contracting were clarified and resolved. Supervisors and employees were now fully accountable for how the work was assigned, with amazing results in productivity achieved in a very short time.

Poor Preventive Maintenance

The supervisor of preventive maintenance, in conjunction with his staff, redesigned their work and created a long-term schedule for prevention. They now functioned as a team in the resolution of critical preventive maintenance issues.

Wasting of Public Funds

There was no wasting of public funds within the department. However, a lengthy discussion occurred between management and grounds staff regarding the necessity to utilize outside contractors on some facilities. In maintenance, a new project management format was put in place that asked supervisors, the estimator, and the scheduler to evaluate each job for more effective utilization of existing staff, rather than contracting out all larger projects. It was determined that there were ways to legitimately and creatively perform requisition and capital improvement projects to up the rate of requisition return.

Poor Safety Habits and Unsafe Working Conditions

In most cases, the issues raised by the employees were addressed at the time of the intervention. What had changed was sharing with the employees what new equipment had been requested in the fixed asset process. Issues such as fire safety and the poor condition of equipment were discussed and resolved. The employees, however, had to address issues of safety unclean work spaces and poor tool maintenance. Informing and including the employees in discussions reduced the belief that safety was not a priority of the department and its managers.

Understaffed and Overworked Custodial Division

New employees were hired during the intervention to bring the complement of employees up to the requirement. There still were not as many employees on board as staff would have liked, but supervisors and managers believed that restructuring the work would effectively resolve the problem.

Undersupplied Personnel

A review of the warehouse and purchasing requirements suggested that undersupplying was not a real issue. However, it appeared that stocked items were not necessarily the desired items. Management instituted a new automated warehousing system that significantly influenced inventory control management and purchasing of desired equipment for the future. Standardization of some areas (such as paint colors) significantly assisted in reducing complaints about undersupply and overall stress. Employees were allowed the flexibility of ordering stock items, within budget, that they believed would allow them to perform their work more effectively.

Poor Employee Communication

The entire intervention process improved the communication cycle for all employees. The skills learned were being used daily throughout the department.

Nepotism and Favoritism

No evidence of nepotism existed within the department. The issue was raised in the grounds division when it was thought that a cousin of the superintendent was hired and that the superintendent directed the relative's work assignments. This was not the case. The employee did not report to the superintendent, and, moreover, the employee was not a relative but a close friend. Favoritism appeared based on performance criteria; not because one employee was liked over another. To alleviate this concern, work was assigned more evenly, and training standards were upgraded to ensure that all employees within a classification could perform the assignments of that classification.

Refrigerators

Employees felt that refrigerators were removed as a retaliatory reaction by the maintenance and construction superintendent. Whether it was retaliation or not is a moot issue. The removal was poor timing and poor judgment on the part of the department. To remedy the situation, risk management was asked to review the areas for safety-related issues and determined that refrigerators for the employees were not a problem. Therefore, three refrigerators were purchased using the assistant administrative officer's budget and placed in the shops.

Dispatcher

It was determined that a dispatcher would significantly assist the supervisors in the performance of their duties in the maintenance division. A classification description was designed by the consultant, including all rationale, and forwarded to classification for review and implementation.

Personnel-Related Matters

It was determined that four employees were working out of class for a period of two years. A request was made by the consultant to classification to upgrade their positions. Numerous other requests for the positions of fire technician, general maintenance worker II, administrative services manager, and building services superintendent as well as pay band changes for custodial chief, deputy director, and other classifications were forwarded to classification by the department for action. A conflict between the maintenance and construction superintendent and an employee's spouse were resolved. An employee dispute with the labor relations personnel officer regarding classification description conflict was resolved. An employee and supervisor conflict was resolved regarding vacation/sick time usage. Numerous conflicts within maintenance—issues involving plumbers, mechanics, painters, boiler plant operators, warehouse, custodial, supervisor/manager, and employee/board—were also resolved.

ORGANIZATIONAL DEVELOPMENT SUMMARY

This chapter describes the organizational development intervention within the Facilities Management Department of Southern California County provided by the consulting firm of Lloyd C. Williams and Associates. The chapter details the methodology used for data collection and analysis, the theoretical perspective of the consultant for responding to the issues of the department, the varying recommendations critical to the success of the organization, the documents and training programs provided to the employees of the department, a list of issues resolved during the intervention, and the existing issues to be resolved. The following sections depict continuing issues within the department and a prognosis for success should all recommendations be implemented. I also try to identify existing problems outside the scope of this contract for consideration by the department and the Public Works assistant administrative officer.

This organizational development intervention did not focus on the symptoms of the department but on the underlying causes of the dysfunctions that occurred creating long-standing organizational symptoms. It was essential that Facilities Management not fall prey to the symptoms created by hurt, trauma, power, authority, rules, regulations, procedures, or historical precedents. True healing of wounds, leadership of employees, and effective management of work require a commitment to creating an environment in which each individual is capable of achieving his or her potential. The former system within Facilities Management did not allow managers or employees to realize their potential for personal success and organizational fulfillment. Through increased awareness, enhanced skills, and a collaborative approach to work management, employees and managers were on a new path toward growth and change.

The road to continued success is not complete. There are still issues within the department that can impede long-term success, a discussion of which follows.

CONTINUING ISSUES

Systems change is a never-ending process for organizations. It requires an organization to constantly reexamine the effectiveness of structural, procedural, or process alterations. The change is balanced by the organization's ability to continue to restructure based on emerging needs. Such was the case with Facilities Management. All changes recommended in this chapter existed for a given period in time. Change, by its very nature, is not static; therefore, the responsibility for constant review was the direct and sole responsibility of Marie Vasquez, director of Facilities Management. Each employee was accountable for ensuring the success of the organization and for recommending changes that benefited the organizational mission. However, systems change through policies, procedures, and administrative management must remain the responsibility of the director.

Throughout this process, it was interesting to observe and follow the responses of employees. The old adage "Be careful about what you ask for; you might get it" played a significant role in the outcome of this intervention. Employees must recognize that there are positive and negative costs to the requests made for change. In this situation, some might see more work as a negative cost, while others might see shared responsibility and accountability as a positive cost. In either case, what changed was the way work was accomplished, when that work was identified and accomplished, who did that work, and how that work was done.

The critical issue was accepting personal and organizational responsibility without blaming someone else. Change meant that mistakes would be made and that nothing was static. Only through teamwork, collaboration, effective decision making, building of better relationships, better understanding of the system, and effective problem resolution would the organization continue to move forward.

Existing Problems

Maintenance

There continued to be a significant deficiency in the skills and abilities of the maintenance supervisors. It was felt that significant work needed to occur within this group to ensure overall success of the maintenance division. Additionally, maintenance groups throughout the region developed attitudes boarding on "prima donna." It was essential that maintenance employees recognize their roles as team members, not prima donnas, if total success were to occur.

Grounds

More time needed to be spent by the grounds superintendent developing his two supervisors. Significant improvement had occurred through his efforts, but more work needed to occur one on one to ensure a skill equity among these three persons.

Custodial

The custodial division continued to perform well. The custodial chief and the deputy director had worked on their relationship. The custodial chief was working on altering his style of functioning to work more effectively with the deputy director. Although this was progressing nicely, more still needed to be done. Employees needed to recognize that more creativity on their part would solidify the work scope and reduce stressors in crunch periods.

Warehouse

It was hoped that changing the reporting structure, automating the services of the department, and proceduralizing the functions would significantly improve the functioning of the warehouse staff with the other divisions of the department.

Home Repair

The supervisor of home repair needs to spend more time upgrading his skills in coaching, counseling, and performance management. This enhancement would significantly improve his performance in the management of the work and leadership of the employees under his charge.

External Issues

Policy Concerns

There was a concern that some congruence matching needed to occur between the differing policies of Southern California County and the

Facilities Management Department. Policies are the guiding tenets of organizational planning and implementation strategies. In the case of Facilities Management, desired outcomes had impacted departmental policy versus county policy. It was therefore suggested that negotiations occur between the assistant administrative officer of public works, the county administrative officer, and the department director to co-create an organizational match that met the needs of both the department and the county. Existing policy made total congruence difficult for the Facilities Management Department.

Organizational Intervention Outcome Perspective

The intervention with the Facilities Management Department focused on the co-creation of strategies that made sense for the employees and the management team. The critical issue was the creation of a trust-oriented environment that allowed management and employees to believe that change could happen. The culture of the organization began to change based on recognition that blame and shame were ineffective strategies. Management had to stop blaming employees, employees had to stope blaming management, and both sides had to recognize that their effectiveness was based on mutual work toward a successful outcome.

ORGANIZATIONAL VIOLENCE: AN AWAKENING PROCESS

Within two weeks of finishing the consultation with the Facilities Management Department, I began to recognize that a very critical assessment and intervention process had not occurred with the client. It was difficult to assess because I was used to addressing the traditional issues of organizational dysfunction. What I had overlooked was the underlying violence paradigm that guided a lot of the actions of the managers and the employees. I began to see that two paradigms co-existed. The existing organizational paradigm focused on Southern California County's historical perspective of performing work. Also, each time management or employees experienced a level of trauma or hurt, the second, underlying violence paradigm became stronger. The violence paradigm grew each time employees felt excluded, each time managers believed that employees were deliberately discounting their attempts to change and work with employees, each time managers or employees believed that the other group rationalized strategies that hurt the other, and each time new bonds or relationships were severed. In effect, I had missed an opportunity to address a critical paradigm that governed the actions of the organization.

I quickly began to reexamine the intervention with the organization and recognized that, by instinct, I had performed some of the necessary actions critical to expunging violence. However, I had not performed all of the necessary actions critical to eradicating violence. Because I had missed some critical issues, I knew that the problems addressed in the consultation could raise their heads again.

Continued Intervention with Facilities Management

I have continued consultation with the Facilities Management Department. Current strategies are focusing on the creation of standards that assist in bridging the issues of violence within the organization. Systems, rules, appearance, and practice standards are making a difference in the department's ability to reshape a future that values, empowers, and supports continual change toward identified outcomes that matter to employees, managers, and the organization as a whole.

As a team, we have begun to identify the historical tenets of violence that have been a part of the organization for many years. Critical to the success of the expanded intervention is remembering how easily blame and shame became major factors for blocking successful bonding, inclusion, empowerment, and ownership by all members of the department. Also important to the success of the expanded intervention has been assessing the control and influence factors that have kept the organization from creating standards, as well as the creation of a systematic approach to change around the violence paradigm. No longer has the approach been a haphazard trial-and-error process; rather, it has emerged as a systematic approach to change through blending needs, wants, and goals with strategies and techniques for creating balance and support.

THE FUTURE

The future of the Facilities Management Department of Southern California County is predicated on the tenets of this book. The next few chapters explain in both overview and step-by-step fashion how organizations can work toward and achieve their outcomes without violence.

Part Three

The Prescription for Change

8

Building the Prescription for
Expunging Violence

The process of expunging violence from organizations is a complex process. Yet the strategy to begin the process of change is a very systematic approach. In each of the cases in the previous four chapters, violence was an underlying issue that was not addressed by the decision makers of the organization, or by me as a consultant in chapter seven. What became apparent to me in my annual review of consultation and in my discussions with persons involved in all the cases was the failure to recognize the violence prevalent in the organizations. Each of the cases was analyzed by the decision makers from the standpoint of management and leadership theory, organizational theories, and some components of systems theory. None of the approaches addressed the issue of violence, and none of the strategies traditionally used in organizational development intervention was effective for the situations expressed in the cases.

To effectively assess the issues of violence, a cursory look at management and systems issues is important. Systems are organized approaches to addressing relationships between the parts or elements of the system. Systems are composed of five basic characteristics. The first characteristic of a system is its *descriptive elements*, or how it is described. The element of description can be the system's nature of work, its product, or a given boundary of the system. In the case of the Northeast Test Preparation Center (see chapter six), elements that described the organization were testing outcomes, geographic facilities, policies and procedures of the organization, human resources, and so forth. All of these elements can be articulated as separate pieces of the whole. The second characteristic of a system is its *boundaries*. A boundary is any organizational component that creates breaks between the elements of the system. Again, using the test center as an example, its boundaries included the differing rules between its remote facilities and the parent company in New York. The third characteristic of the system is the *relationship process*. The relationships occurring within the system identify associations that exist, such as the interactions of the human resources, the levels of power within the system, or the commonalities of structures within the system. The fourth characteristic is the *quality component* of the system, which describes the system in its entirety, which may be different from its parts. In government, providing service is a quality of the entire system; enforcement of land-use rules, provision of testing rules, and service delivery of welfare benefits are all qualities of the individual elements of the system. They are all different yet reflect the overall quality of the whole. *Causes* are the final component of systems. Causes are the reasons for actions or changes within the system. The dynamic of working together is the process that keeps all characteristics of a system in check and together.

Thus, every organization is a system composed of descriptive elements, boundaries, relationships, qualities, and causes. Every organization creates its own definition of being or working in the world. In effect, every organization creates its own paradigm. Recent thought defines the shift that occurs from one paradigm to another as *paradigm reconstruction*. Paradigm shifts are not as common as management and consultants would believe; rather, paradigm shifts are total system alterations based on changes made to one or more components of the existing system. Violence is often the outcome when a dramatic shift begins to occur within the organization that alters the original world view of that organization. When management changes the structures or the processes or any one or several of the elements of the organization the expressed changes can create a shift toward violence. Policies that alter the quality of the organization cause the violence paradigm.

Consider an organization that is trying to downsize in order to remain competitive. The process of downsizing does not necessarily change the organization's descriptive elements, rather that the boundaries that originally separated the elements may be changing to fit one set of reasons or another. The boundary change itself may not be the issue but application of the process used by the organization may be inappropriate. Violence occurs because misunderstanding of altering processes, or being incongruent with processes, creates mistrust of all aspects of systems. Utilizing management techniques, leadership techniques, or other strategies does not address the real underlying issue of organizational dysfunction. Certainly, one can make changes in the rules or the structure in an attempt to make things better. Unfortunately, if the process of trauma and pain has already begun, none of the management or organizational development techniques will positively affect organization, nor will resolution of the violence occur through traditional strategies.

I began to look at the essential components of expunging violence as a process of *system creation*. The first step was understanding the components of the violence system or paradigm, which are:

1. the tenets of violence, such as bonding factors and power factors;
2. the vessels of violence, such as policies, rules, and labor agreements;
3. the structure of violence, such as the lack of systems, rules, appearance, and practice standards;
4. the process of violence, such as circles of control versus circles of influence parameters; and
5. the boundaries of violence, such as balance of power strategies.

Each of these components can be set in motion by violation of the characteristics of any existing system. The violence paradigm is therefore in existence at all times with any other system or paradigm. Figure 8.1 depicts the relationship of the existing organizational system as the dominant system with the violence paradigm as a sublevel system just below the existing organizational system. It is important to remember that both systems exist at all times. The issue becomes ensuring that the violence paradigm does not rear its head and become the dominant system within the organization.

As the violence paradigm operates in tandem with all other paradigms, it becomes important to understand the "hook" or "trigger" that allows the violence paradigm to become the primary paradigm in the system. The trigger for the violence paradigm is the lack of a vacuum in the system. Each time a shift occurs in the components of systems, a vacuum-like situation is needed for the organization to assimilate that shift through learning. That vacuum becomes the most critical component for suppressing the violence paradigm. For example, management may thrust a policy it has been keeping under wraps upon an employee at the last minute, demanding a change in the employee's life. Another example is when one partner in a relationship announces a surprise change in the nature of the relationship to the other partner. Each time an organization creates a shift within the organizational system without attending to the wholeness of the process of change (e.g., consulting employees about the change), the violence paradigm is triggered and becomes superimposed on the existing system, as depicted in Figure 8.2.

Figure 8.1
Coexistent Paradigms

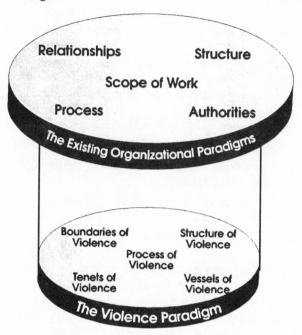

In the case of the Southern California County consultation, I did not realistically address the violence paradigm *at the same time* that I was altering other paradigms within the organization. I was thereby enabling the violence paradigm to be superimposed on all consultation intervention in progress. To have been more effective in the consultation, I would have needed to evaluate all six tenets of the violence paradigm. Had bonding been created, or could bonds be built between management and employees to ensure that some levels of trust were created between levels? Had the process of growth been an inclusive process? Was everyone affected involved? Had the need for empowerment of the individual been balanced by the need for empowerment of the team? Were new ideas and ideals embraced or discounted? Were existing issues of power, control, and authority resolved? Was an assessment made of ends justifying the means? Many aspects of this analysis occurred; however, what is unique about the violence paradigm is that *all* aspects must be evaluated to prevent the superimposition from occurring.

In the Southern California County consultation, all the *vessels of violence* must be evaluated in relation to the tenets of violence. Do the policies, procedures, administrative regulations, labor agreements, hiring practices, organizational structures, and supervisory processes inhibit the

Figure 8.2
Superimposed Violence Paradigm

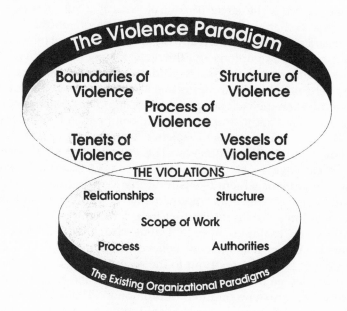

tenets of violence from thriving, or do the vessels of violence actualize
the thriving of the tenets of violence? Again, the analysis must look at
all of the vessels. Even if the analysis focuses on the training of employees, it is important to assess all the vessels in relation to the outcomes
of the training.

Most important to evaluating the coexistence of the violence paradigm
with other paradigms is analyzing the *structures of violence*. Does the
organization have existing systems standards, rules standards, appearance standards, and practice standards? Herein lies the most difficult
issue for managers, leaders, or consultants to evaluate. It is difficult for
organizations or persons to assess the congruence of thoughts and actions. The process of evaluation should be close to an empirical analysis
in ensuring that rationalizations or discounts are not prevalent to bias
the analysis. The process of evaluating standards requires just such an
approach. The purpose of the standards analysis is to set the stage for
expunging the violence. The structure of violence within the organization is the key to expunging the violence, the basis from which system
alterations must be made.

The *process of violence* is the next point of analysis. Based on the operations of the organization, are circles of control or circles of influence

governing thought and action within organizational life? Analysis of the process of violence within organizations often suggests that organizations operate from the circle of control. This is a critical factor in the organizational change process. Where the circle of control is the rule, the *boundaries of violence* interrupt organizational life. Herein lies the reason for creation of unions and the reawakening of collective bargaining. The boundaries of violence focus on strategies to place in check the existing behaviors of organizations that are perceived as violent by those oppressed. When the violence paradigm is dominant, balance of power, freedoms of association, and incongruent competition become the strategies for change. The tenets of violence focus on strategies to enhance the relationships with employees. The critical issue is balancing the needs of employees with the needs of the organization. Essential to effective tenet management is ensuring that both employees and management are successful. All components of the violence paradigm must be addressed in a coexistent manner in order to expunge violence.

Consider, for example, an organization struggling with the concept of diversity. Upper management believes that affirmative action goals and strategies are very important to the success of the organization, but employees may be used to and comfortable with the existing paradigm that places a high value on internal promotion. The organization's approach to change demands a radical shift in hiring and promotion techniques that violates the existing values of the organization. The struggle in this change is balancing the value of diversity with the value of promotion from within. How management embraces the shift in the organizational paradigm determines the dominance of the violence paradigm. A less thought-out approach would bring the violence paradigm to the forefront.

Another example occurred during a weeklong intellectual seminar for organizational consultants. The process was designed to allow us to embrace intellectual inquiry and research as tantamount to scholar-practitioner development. An important goal of the process was to challenge ourselves to create new knowledge. In one of the sessions, the notion of using an Afrocentric paradigm of knowledge creation was proposed. The instructor stated that only Eurocentrism was acceptable unless one disproved the value of Eurocentric thinking in the research. Then and only then could Afrocentric thinking be utilized and valued by the research community. The notion and the messenger were then dismissed and discounted. At that moment, the violence paradigm began to dominate the sessions. When the same instructor dismissed the childrearing methods of Western women because they did not meet the value-laden standards of Third World mothers, the violence paradigm was entrenched in the minds of many of the participants, for collaborative, innovative, and creative knowledge creations were being attacked. The vessels of violence abounded, and the instructor never invested the energy to ensure that the tenets of violence were managed. The discount of ideas and ideals became the predominant tenet of violence in the process.

All members of any system—whether they are managers, consultants, professors, co-workers, or family members—participate in the dominance of the violence paradigm. This is not because they want to experience violence but because little attention is given to ensuring that the violence paradigm remains at a sublevel of organizational life. So how do we work through a process of violence when it has occurred? How do we traverse the waters of change without initializing the violence paradigm?

To assist with looking at the process of expunging violence from organizations, consider the case of a small engineering consulting firm. Marc, the owner of the firm, recently retired from active service in the firm but decided to ensure the survivability of the firm by becoming the chair of the board of directors. He fashioned himself as a disciplined engineer focused toward environmental engineering concerns. Throughout his tenure as president, he had always had his hands in all facets of the company to determine that no violations of regulations would occur in the work that the company performed. It was his belief that he must be certain that all work was accurate, thereby ensuring that the reputation of the firm would grow. Marc was correct in his assumptions about the firm, and its reputation had grown enormously with contracts generating $4 million in annual profits.

David, the engineering firm's new manager, believed that more sales could be generated with the hiring of more environmentally sensitive engineers. He recognized that the historical perspective of the firm involved the hiring of persons like Marc, strong-willed and expert in specific disciplines. However, as the new manager, David was committed to hiring more generalized engineers, minorities, and women to promote different levels of contracting from the company's existing clients. Almost immediately, David began to experience resistance from the other managers. They were not specific in their objections but only expressed their feelings and discomforts. David felt that these were forms of pseudoresistance because the objections were not specific. He pressed on toward his desired outcomes. Within one month, David recognized that something was not right. The managers and the employees were complaining about the process that David was using to create change. The managers felt that David was making changes unilaterally. They resented his attitude that he had all the answers. They also felt that he was too new in his role, although they had known him for fifteen years. He was changing, and they didn't like it. David felt there was some validity to their complaints, but creating a diverse organization that could take on new challenges outweighed what he saw as the managers' short-sighted approach. So David pushed on.

Four months passed, and Marc called David into his office. Marc was terminating David's services as manager and his employment with the company. Marc's rationale was that David had created too much up-heaval in the company, and someone was needed in that position who would carry on the old traditions of the organization. David was mor-tified. He received his severance check and left the company.

Severely depressed, David went to see a clinical/organizational psy-chologist to help him sort out the issues. The psychologist said that David had not attended to the business of the organization or of the employees in his desire to promote change. The psychologist told David that he had created a violent organization and that the employees had defeated him through the boundaries of violence. David was confused and felt it was important to understand how this had occurred so that he could prevent it in the future. The psychologist explained that the old organization was a congruent one based on the owner instituting very clear, linear goals within the organization for controlling a segment of the market. The process had worked well, and the owner probably hired managers who would toe the line in accordance with his views. The process had worked, and employees felt comfortable because they knew what to expect. The rules and processes were clearly defined, and the expertise allowed each to contribute based on disciplined comfort. When David took the reins, he devalued the history of the organization, yet he used the style of the owner to implement change. He violated the tenets of change by superimposing a violence paradigm on the or-ganization. He needed to attend to the creation of relationships and bonds with his colleagues because his role had changed. He needed to share his outcomes, include them in the decision-making process, and listen to the individual needs of the managers. Unfortunately, he did not perform in that manner, so the employees believed that the stan-dards of the organization were being discounted for David's personal needs. With that in mind, collaboration, problem resolution, and com-munication were replaced by balance of power approaches, freedoms of association, and incongruent competition on the part of the managers. What had existed within the organization was replaced by the group's need to create equity. The choice, then, was to expunge David while maintaining equity and the historical organization. What David had not understood was that his approach to the existing organization was con-sistent with past changes, but his lack of attention to the tenets of vi-olence had set in motion a battle to rebuild what was comfortable for everyone else within the organization. David had misread the organi-zation, and that had cost him his job.

Often the process of violence is the underlying factor in choices made by organizations, and, like David, employees or managers, often do not understand the driving force behind their thoughts and actions. Attending to the process of violence is critical for successful change or maintenance of an organization. The next chapter discusses a step-by-step approach to expunging the violence.

9

Expunging Organizational Violence: A Step-by-Step Assessment Process

The previous five chapters focus on examples of violence created in different organizations. Each chapter identifies that organizations choose to shift the paradigm that governed their functioning in one facet or another. That shift triggers the violence paradigm from a coexistent state to a dominant state in organizational interaction and functioning. What inevitably occurs is organizational change through management strategies without acknowledgment of the violence paradigm's existence or its influence on the course of organizational development. To effectively change the dynamics within the organizations, simultaneous assessment of both the organization and the potential for violence is required.

THE DISEMPOWERING PROCESS: HOW THE VIOLENCE PARADIGM BEGINS

A step-by-step approach to understanding the creation, coexistence, and elimination of the violence paradigm involves looking at how organizations create a new product or service. Initially, organizations determine that a change is required in the service or product line based on outside competition or quality-of-life issues in the community. This process often involves rethinking the strategic objectives or the political realities that significantly influence the direction of the organization. In any case, the "power" of the instigator for change establishes the framework for the violence paradigm to begin the superimposing process (refer back to Figures 8.1 and 8.2).

Take, for example, a new commissioner within a county government. The commissioner was elected on a platform of increasing the diversity of the decision makers within the organization. The commissioner met with the county administrative officer during her first week in office, dictating that change would occur or the county administrative officer would be voted out of his position. The commissioner was singularly focused on fulfilling a campaign pledge of the inclusion of minorities and/or women to decision-making roles and was unconcerned with any other factors that might affect change.

The county administrative officer recognized the force behind the commissioner's directive and created a plan of attack to carry out the commissioner's directive. This is step one of the violence paradigm. The paradigm began because a request for change has been made and action is focused only on the change. Step one is to determine all the details, or the full scope of the work, involved in carrying out the commissioner's plan. The first step in the creation of the violence paradigm occurs because, although the full scope of work is planned to carry out the commissioner's directive, other matters are neglected. To define the full work scope, the county administrative officer looked at the desired outcome—hiring minority and female decision makers—and then assessed what resources were required and what time frame was necessary to achieve it. Upon assessing the scope, the county administrative officer also factored into the equation the political realities and the strategic perspectives. These were all *conscious assessments* of step one in the process, but *unconscious assessments* were also occurring based on changes created by the county administrative officer and the commissioner.

Figure 9.1 indicates that a desired outcome is a product of not only the conscious assessment of time, resources, and scope but also the Six Box Process of unconscious assessment. In effect, the components of the six boxes are equally important to the successful change process. When any one of the unconscious components is overlooked or discounted in the planning process, the violence paradigm begins.

Every employee within the organization begins to trust the organization based on the organization's ability to consistently implement the six components of unconscious assessment, not the components of conscious assessment. The implementation program that employees recognize includes policies, procedures, administrative regulations, and organizational practice. The unconscious components are the daily actions of employees that guide their experiences of violence or nonviolence. Contrary to the beliefs of most management theorists, the vessels of violence are discounted by employees until they have begun to experience the tenets of violence. Then, the vessels of violence are assessed by employees as objects of disdain. Therefore, when the county administrative officer created a change without assessing the impact on policy,

Figure 9.1
Step One: Creating the Violence Paradigm

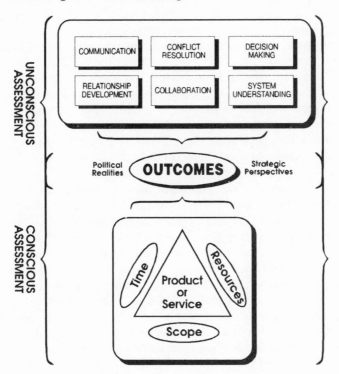

procedure, or practice—the vessels of violence—the violence paradigm begin. The employees experienced inconsistency, and the inconsistency triggered a lack of trust and confidence, feelings of unfairness, and, in extreme situations, blame and shame. Employees saw the change as an issue of management control.

Looking back to chapter three, Figure 3.1 shows the control process as experienced by employees. When the change occurs without attending to the unconscious assessment issues, the circle of control expands. The circle of control is I-oriented; those operating within this circle act for the good of self, not the whole. The more control is expanded, the more employees within the organization experience mistrust, miscommunication, inconsistency, incongruence, politics, incompetence, and combative behavior. In effect, the expansion of the circle of control is a process of disempowerment.

Returning to the previous example, the county administrative officer's desire to meet the commissioner's requirements set in motion step one of the violence paradigm. The lack of attention to the unconscious assessments initiated the expansion of the circle of control. Employees began to experience the tenets of violence. There was no attempt to ensure that effective bonds existed among the employees affected by the change, no inclusion of the employees in developing strategies to meet the needs of the commissioner, no attempt to balance individuality with teamwork or team change, no attempt to resolve the problem of increased control or authority on the part of the commissioner, and no discussion about the ends justifying the means. Instead, unilateral choices (decision making at the top) were made that did not assess the organizational health of employees to embrace change. Many would say that tough choices often breed violence and that change sometimes requires violence as an appropriate means to a justified end. I disagree with that premise. Change is successful because of careful attention to the tenets of violence.

Step two of the violence paradigm occurs when anyone affected by the change requests clarification regarding the outcomes desired within the change process. When clarification is requested, but the answer given comes from within the circle of control, the violence paradigm is escalated. In step one, the tenets and vessels of violence are experienced by employees; in step two, the structure and process of violence are what escalate the system. The structure of violence is composed of the varying standards that impact organizational functioning. In the case of the violence paradigm, standards are usually nonexistent. The situation with the county administrative officer illustrates this process. Political realities often suggest that change must occur irrespective of the system in operation. The commissioner stated that she wanted change or heads would roll. In effect, the intrusion of political reality violated whatever standards existed. In a nonviolent system, employees were assured that standards of operation were in place. If the employee discovered that standards did not exist, then the structure of violence would occur. In this case, the employees would look for four standards: the system standard, the rules standard, the appearance standard, and the practice standard.

The system standard is the consistent development of political policy. Regardless of the identified outcomes of political decision making, politics follows a structural approach to change. There is usually some attention given to balancing the needs of constituents to create an aura of calm within organizational action. The aura of calm is the critical ingredient of system standards. Calm is created by the incremental process of change. All the palms are greased and all the rough spots are rounded before the changes are implemented. In the case of the commissioner and the county administrative officer, the aura of calm was discounted, thus creating an aura of chaos. What was normal for the system standard was overlooked by the drive for change.

The rules standard is the consistent development of organizational policy. It is the gauge of the organization that builds credibility by consistency and equity in the policies, written regulations, departmental operating procedures, and all standing orders. The rules standard is critical because employees build faith and trust on the idea that the organization has their best interests at heart through equitable application of the rules. Regardless of the nuances that can occur within organizations, consistent application of the rules—policies, procedures, and regulations—maintains an aura of calm. Each time an action occurs that is different from stated or written policy, an aura of chaos is created. The rules are usually created to provide a framework for performance, action, and control. Employees understand those controls because they existed prior to their joining the organization. Even if the controls change during an employee's tenure with the organization, calm can be maintained because changes in rules are usually incremental. When the county administrative officer made changes without utilizing the existing rules, an aura of chaos was the outcome.

The appearance standard is the consistent and congruent image portrayed to employees and the public that suggests fairness and equity in all actions of the organization. The appearance standard is the gauge of the organization essential to the establishment of trust. Consistency and congruence are critical to the survivability of the appearance standard. When an organization appears to be something it's not, mistrust and discomfort result. The objective of the appearance standard is to create a sense of morality in the actions of the organization. For example, if a community values fairness in responding to the homeless situation, yet its laws prohibit sleeping in the park, application of the rule might violate the appearance standard. One can be legally right and morally wrong, or vice versa; appearance is the key to that consistency and congruence.

The practice standard is the gauge of day-to-day functioning that demonstrates adherence to the appearance, rules, and system standards of the organization. If the organization states that it values and empowers employees, yet employees are on the receiving end of power, control, and manipulation, then the practice standard is counterproductive to the rules, appearance, and system standards. An aura of chaos is established, dichotomous to the expressions of the organization.

Violations of the standards create the structure of violence. The county administrative officer violated all the standards by trying to please the commissioner. That is not to say that the commissioner's goal of diversity within the organization was not admirable; rather, that the process utilized to accomplish the desired outcome caused violence within the organization. Ultimately, continued inconsistent and incongruent behavior by an organization superimposes the violence paradigm on any existing organizational paradigm (refer back to Figure 8.2).

Once the violence paradigm is superimposed on the existing organization, step three occurs. Step three implements the process of violence and the boundaries of violence. When affected persons sense that standards are nonexistent within the organization, all attention becomes focused on the processes of violence. The process of violence occurs through movement from the circle of influence toward the circle of control. This movement occurs because an aura of chaos takes control of the organizational environment. The circle of control is actualized by the concept of inconsistency and incongruence. I-oriented actions or self-serving acts become prevalent, suggesting that looking out for others is of very low value and protectionist behavior is necessary. All actions are suspect; all behavior is mistrustful; all statements seem to have hidden meaning; and teamwork, collaboration, and we-oriented actions dissipate.

Let's return to our example of county government in the midst of the process of violence. To recap, the chief administrative officer (CAO) has received orders from the county commissioner regarding increasing minorities and females in decision-making roles within the government. The CAO, through negotiations with assistant administrative officers (AAOs), alters the recruitment process for four key department director positions. The CAO and the AAOs agree that they will quietly recruit for minorities. They contact people they know in the industry, select a number of potential minority candidates, and interview them for the positions.

David and Susan are senior managers within county government. They were counting on an opportunity to interview for these key positions. They have worked hard in the organization, each having been with the organization for ten years. They have paid their dues, in their minds, and feel that they have developed the expertise required to be successful in the more responsible role of department director. The standards of the organization have always supported promotion from within. But rumor has it that the positions must be filled by minorities from outside the organization. They realize that this implies that they have no chance; however, history says that promotion from within is the appearance standard.

The CAO interviews David and Susan for department director positions. The next day, he announces the selection of four minority candidates from outside the organization to fill the positions. The commissioner is pleased with the selections, and the CAO feels that David and Susan will understand. The CAO is wrong. David and Susan jointly request a meeting with the CAO demanding an explanation of the selection process. This process of pleading starts the dysfunctional communication cycle (see Figure 9.2). The CAO hears their concern and begins to explain his rationale for selection. David and Susan display their anger and hurt at the choice and say that they were discounted

Figure 9.2
The Processes of Violence

COMMUNICATION DYSFUNCTION

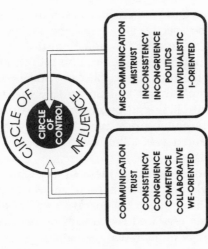

SYSTEMS FOCUS

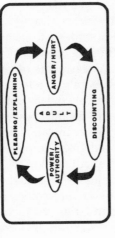

CONTROL SYSTEM

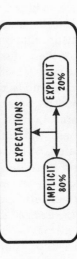

CIRCLE OF INFLUENCE

CIRCLE OF CONTROL

COMMUNICATION	MISCOMMUNICATION
TRUST	MISTRUST
CONSISTENCY	INCONSISTENCY
CONGRUENCE	INCONGRUENCE
COMETENCE	POLITICS
COLLABORATIVE	INDIVIDUALISTIC
WE-ORIENTED	I-ORIENTED

EXPECTATIONS CYCLE

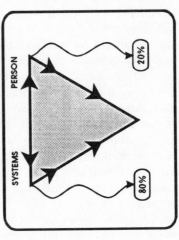

EXPECTATIONS

IMPLICIT 80%

EXPLICIT 20%

and that the CAO caved in to political pressure. The CAO, unaccustomed to challenges from staff, takes a stance of power and authority, stating that it is his decision and that David and Susan must accept his actions or leave. With the process of dysfunctional communication firmly underway, the circle of control begins.

The circle of control operates from a perspective of self-serving behavior, which demands a winner and a loser. The I-oriented person is unclear in communication and behaves inconsistently, altering behavior to ensure that only one perspective is valued or heard. When David and Susan were discounted, all communication from the organization became suspect, all behavior from the organization became mistrustful, all policies and actions of the organization became incongruent, and all standards became political. David and Susan saw the actions of the organization as very controlling and punitive. Their expectations, that fairness and equity were guiding principles of the organization, were violated. What they wanted was adherence to standards; what they found were no standards.

Because the organization devalued them by selecting different department directors, David and Susan became subject to the *boundaries of violence*. David and Susan began to look at strategies to balance the actions of the CAO. They reviewed the vessels of violence—the rules, policies, procedures, and administrative regulations. They found a lack of adherence to equity, fairness, and equal opportunity in hiring practices and promotion policies and other standards of operational policy, which they noted for use in pressing their case. David and Susan then contacted an attorney. They talked of a strategy to balance the power of the CAO and the commissioner. They focused their energy on addressing the control. The unconscious assessments of communication, conflict resolution, decision making, collaboration, relationship building, and understanding the system were overlooked; David and Susan were on a different mission—creating power to balance power.

In that short experience, the existing organizational paradigm had become dominated by the violence paradigm. No movement could be made with David and Susan without first addressing the elimination of the violence. They were emotionally and professionally stuck in the process of violence. The CAO and the commissioner soon began to experience other components of the boundaries of violence. Using freedom of associations and incongruent competition, David and Susan contacted the unions, the media, and the other commissioners to put pressure on the CAO and the commissioner. The CAO and the commissioner found themselves embroiled in an appearance, rules, and system standards issue of immense proportion. The aura of chaos was in full force, and the good brought on by the hiring of minorities was overshadowed by the violent process created to implement the organizational change. Organizational miscommunication, mistrust, inconsistent performance, incongruent action, and politics became the new norm. The media said the organization was self-serving (I-oriented). All four minorities resigned and filed lawsuits against the county. Everyone was losing.

Many times people try to do the right thing, for the right cause, but through the wrong process. The degree of anger experienced because of this has nothing to do with the overall plan or objective; it is a result of the process used to achieve that objective. Such is the case with the violence paradigm. In each of the steps to this point, the rationale or overall strategy was not at issue; the process was the catalyst for the violence. Therefore, the violence paradigm is a process paradigm. The process coexists with other elements, but the violence paradigm emerges as dominant in reaction to the processes placed in motion. For example, President George Bush was not necessarily wrong in the strategies he created to assist the United States in achieving economic health; it was his process that people disagreed with. President Bill Clinton may not have more effective plans than the previous administration, but many people have more trust in his process. By appealing to the middle class—that is, the masses—in his economic pledges, Clinton's approach to systems/societal change seems less violent.

The step-by-step creation of violence is based on a selfish, "my way only" process. When actions taken by business or government affect others, but the others are not included in the development of the strategy, violence becomes the real outcome. The violence occurs because the vacuum that allows each person or each organizational entity to process the impending change is not created. Change is hastily created without valuing bonding, inclusion, and acceptance of others' ideas and ideals. In haste, a system of power, control and authority is created, devoid of equity and equality. We move in haste, taking little time to assess the impacts of our decisions, thereby often creating unjust means to unjust ends. Each time we create these kinds of steps, we embrace the violence paradigm over the process paradigm that is our desired outcome. Dysfunctional communication become the communication of choice. We embrace the circle of control as our operational strategy, and the lack of standards as the methodology for addressing any and all concerns of employees, stakeholders, or the general public. Inconsistency and incongruence are established as the appearance standards. Whether one evaluates classic, dynamic, communication, field, or evolutionary paradigms, discounting the violence paradigm makes successful results impossible.

THE PRESCRIPTIVE PROCESS OF NONVIOLENCE

If the discounting process, circle of control, and lack of standards are key elements of the violence paradigm, then the converse of each of

Figure 9.3
The Nonviolence Paradigm

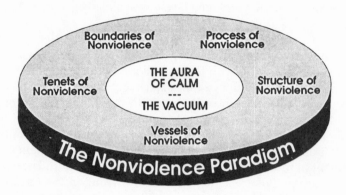

these elements are the key components to a nonviolence paradigm (see Figure 9.3).

The violence paradigm can occur because management pays little attention to ensuring that the tenets of violence are effectively managed in the process of change and maintenance within organizations. Each time a change is considered, management needs to assess the health of the organization, which involves examining the bonds between the employees and the organization. Management may ask these questions: Has the organization been caring toward employees by instituting meaningful and rewarding training programs? Has the organization looked at career paths and promotion strategies? Has the organization instituted employee recognition and involvement programs? Has the leadership of the organization provided opportunities for employees to be heard? Management must also assess the degree to which the organization has involved employees in the planning and decision-making process. Has management looked at a process of inclusion of all employees in the development and implementation of the work scope? Are ideas from employees acknowledged and given serious consideration? Has management conducted employee attitude surveys to discover the real issues employees are concerned about? Has management taken to heart the concerns raised by employees and acted on the issues rather than just give lip service? Has management determined strategies to ensure that the worth and skills of the individual are balanced by the recognition of the team? Has management embraced the strength of the individual in a noncompetitive manner? Has management encouraged multitalented employees to diversify their assignments? Has management drawn on the diversity of employees and their cultural perspectives to provide alternative approaches to problems? Has management prepared the organization to embrace diversity? In effect, has management made employees real and viable partners in the creation, maintenance, and expansion of the organizational system?

Many organizations can answer "yes" to some of the aforementioned questions, but the violence paradigm occurs when the answer to *all* of the questions is not "yes." The violence paradigm is an all-or-nothing paradigm. Addressing each facet of the paradigm is essential to expunging violence. In the case of Southern California County (see chapter 7), I addressed some but not all of the components of the paradigm. One must assess the tenets, vessels, structure, process, and boundaries of violence; without a total approach, the paradigm looms eternal on the organization. Remember that it is a process paradigm, not a structural paradigm. Where violations are discovered, the change process needs to create a vacuum and an aura of calm allowing management and employees to work together to end the violations. The desired outcome of the process is to create standards and a circle of influence (see Figure 9.2).

Management might argue that this takes too much time. They might say an aura of calm would be nice, but competition or political realities will not allow them that luxury. Unfortunately, such discounting of the reality of the paradigm can cost organizations more money through increased employee absences, slowdown of work, and increased union activity. The boundaries of violence—balance of power, freedom of associations, and incongruent competition—grow in direct proportion to the denial of the paradigm by organizational leaders. The issue is not that management is not concerned with the tenets of violence; rather, management does not recognize that the violence paradigm is equally important as anything else occurring within the organization.

So how do we co-manage change and violence? How do we reduce the overall costs involved in a change process? How do we begin to look at nonviolence and work simultaneously? The first step is to rethink the planning process. In chapter one I stated that organizational success is determined by balancing the health of the employees and the organizational congruence of policies, procedures, and practices with the desired outcomes or goals of the organization. Establishing the health of the employees, the congruence of the organizational vessels, and the identification of the outcomes become the first step in expunging violence. Equal assessment and planning for all three components is a critical starting point to a good maintenance or change process.

Examine the health of your own organization. Using a chart might be helpful, incorporating organizational vessels—policies, procedures, rules, and administrative regulations—and the three components of step one. What is the status of the emotional health of the organization? Are targets of lost work time, production, and quality where they should be? Is there a balance between individual performance/recognition and team performance/recognition? On the same chart, look at all the vessels; are they congruent with actual performance? That is, does the organization practice what it preaches? What are the organization's real goals? Based on the chart, determine where there is congruence. If the chart shows that the vessels are inconguent, you will discover that the tenets of violence are in operation, and an aura of calm (the vacuum) is required. To create the aura of calm, any change should be halted so that time is available to repair the existing organizational paradigm. The aura of calm is the critical intervention for organization health. Like the human body, which needs time and rest to heal itself, organizations need the aura of calm to heal. This time can be used to review the tenets of violence and to create a new strategy for bonding, inclusion, listening, embracing difference, and expunging power/control/authority issues. Next, examine how the organization rationalizes and justifies its actions, recognizing that creating a just end is essential to organizational health.

Once the aura of calm is in place and strategies for reparations are underway, then look at the structures of violence. The structures of violence focus on the lack of standards, so to expunge the structures of violence, one must assess the existence of standards within the organization. Earlier in the chapter, it was suggested that organizations are not always cognizant of the four standards that are created—those of system, rules, appearance, and practice. To expunge the violence, a concerted effort is required to create standards. The creation of standards does not destroy creativity; it provides the environment and establishes the organization ethos that guides and governs what we accomplish and the way we accomplish work. Every organization, public, private, or nonprofit, has system standards. The creation of system standards helps in the development of a strategic direction for the organization. Poised in that strategic direction, an organization is can realistically craft rules standards—guiding principles that affect the direction of all policies, procedures, and administrative regulations. This means that negotiated labor agreements, personnel policies, departmental operating procedures, civil service agreements, payroll policies, and supervisory and management rules are all guided by the systems standards; and, as rules standards, they must be congruent. Too often, organizations create policies from the top and violate the policies at every other level. Once each of these areas is assessed and discoveries charted, the three components of the violence paradigm will have been identified. Management is now ready to embrace a system of nonviolence.

The system of nonviolence requires calm in order to impact systems of violence. Effective movement requires recognition of pressures that inhibit organizational change. Peter Berger, author of *Invitation to Sociology: A Humanistic Perspective* (Garden City, NY: Doubleday, 1963), believes that human beings and organizational systems are capable of enormous change and effective direction when they are able to escape the societal definitions placed on them. He says, "the ongoing insurrection of Southern Negroes against the segregated system in our time was similarly preceded by a long process in which the old definitions of their role were discredited in the nation at large and in their own minds. In other words, long before the social systems are brought down in violence, they are deprived of their ideological sustenance by contempt" (p. 130). This statement describes the movement of African-American culture from one span of history to another. Within every organization, employees are often relegated to a specific role, a specific history. The movement to a nonviolent system is movement from one space in history to another—movement from one set of societal, organizational definitions to a new role.

The process of violence is based on the premise that organizations often operate from the circle of control because congruence and clarity are lacking in the vessels and structures of the organization. The process of nonviolence is movement from that circle of control, one specific experience in history, to another, a circle of influence. The experience of a new human resources director of a Fortune 500 company illustrates this shift. The company hired this director to create a new organizational culture within its 100-employee office. The organization believed that it had instituted appropriate organizational vessels to carry out a consistent style of management. However, the new director found that she reported to a vice president who offered a different appearance standard for operating within the organization. Empowerment, inclusion, and embracing difference and newness were not valued by this vice president, in spite of the vessels established by the organization. She sensed that a circle of control, not influence, was the real underlying process of the organization. She therefore opted for continuation of this process to ensure her survivability in the company. Unknowingly perpetuating the process of violence, her tenure was a short 18 months. Afterwards she stated that she should have instituted the process of nonviolence. She was correct in assuming that she was unable to alter the ideological ethos of her vice president and fell prey to the existing organizational history. Where there is a history that appears to be disjointed, one must challenge the efficacy of its existence. The aura of calm must be established to assist in embracing the efficacy of organization history. In the aura of calm, the organization can bring into focus tenets, standards, and vessels so that the process of nonviolence can be undertaken. Consistency, congruence, collaboration, competence, clarity of communication, and trust—all we-oriented approaches—are the tools of the process of nonviolence and the circle of influence (see Figure 9.2). By instituting the circle of influence as the process of nonviolence, more organizational and personal empowerment occurs. This process of empowerment opens the door for the embracing of change.

Once the system of nonviolence is established from the aura of calm, the organization is ready to close the aura of calm and embrace the challenge of change. The final element of violence can now be challenged. The boundary of violence is the last and most visible component. In the 1930s, unions, trade associations, and revolutionary groups were created because organizations created circles of control and violated all the tenets of violence. Balance of power and freedom of associations were awakening as boundaries of violence. Organizations are still trapped in this 1930s mode of behavior because of the lack of a systemic approach to organizational health and congruence. The process of organizational nonviolence is fulfilled in the termination of the boundaries of violence. Organizations creating strategies of inclusion and empowerment reduce the necessity for balance of power, freedom of association, and incongruent competition. Equity and fairness in operations reduce the dominance of power and control. Avenues for hearing the thoughts, feelings, and ideals of others reduce the necessity for the development of associations poised to compete and confront. Avenues for inclusion reduce the competitive necessity of varying groups to speak for the oppressed within organizations.

To be effective in expunging the violence, additional actions should occur beyond understanding the steps in creating a nonviolent paradigm. Primarily, an atmosphere of acceptance among managers needs to be created to look realistically at the style changes necessary for changing systems. In *The Congruence of People and Organizations* (Westport, CT: Quorum Books, 1993), I described differences in the approaches utilized by managers based on the boundaries of their belief structures. The degree to which a manager can embrace all of his or her belief systems affects the ability of the manager to expunge the violence paradigm. An example is the following.

Joe is the chief executive officer of a Fortune 500 company. During the recession of 1988–1991, the company lost the largest share of its market because the company was too rigid in its structure and decision making. The board of directors stated that Joe had to take the company in a new direction. The company had to become more flexible in its structure and in the way it made decisions. This was extremely difficult for Joe. He had taken the Belief Systems Audit in my previous book. The results of the audit showed that Joe had a theological/legal belief system. He liked clear, well-defined boundaries, which helped him maintain a sense of self, and he preferred little chaos and lots of structure. The legal side of Joe's belief system was his stressful side. The legal belief system focuses on power, authority, and control as critical components of one's comfort zone. When Joe felt threatened, unsure, or uncomfortable, he became more authoritarian in his approach. Such was the case in the situation with the board of directors. Rather than embrace the idea of change, Joe felt pressured to participate in a change process that was contrary to his comfort parameters and his style. He procrastinated in carrying out the directive from the board. Joe felt violated, the organization was violated, and change was difficult. The situation experienced by Joe is common when organizations are asked to create change. Lack of clarity about one's boundaries can affect the ability to change. When one's boundaries are threatened or misunderstood, the tenets of violence become superimposed on the initiators of change and therefore on the entire organization. To embrace the paradigm of nonviolence, managers must come to terms with their own boundaries, structures, processes, and tenets. The belief systems create the framework for understanding these elements.

Two simultaneous actions always occur with every action taken within organizations. The first action is the process or what one does; the second action is an assessment of how well one has done with the first action. In the case of creating change, therefore, process alone is not enough. It must be balanced with assessment. Too often, managers only measure process, but in order to be successful, they must measure the quality of the process and the output or service provided. To measure effectively requires balancing the quality of the managers' actions toward human resources with their quality in achieving the overall objectives. Equity is the result of the nonviolence paradigm. Thus, how one performs is equally important to what is performed. David Osborne and Ted Gaebler, in *Reinventing Government* (Reading, MA: Addison-Wesley, 1992, pp. 326–327), state that many factors are critical for fundamental change. They define crisis, leadership, continuity of leadership, healthy civic infrastructure, shared visions and goals, trust, outside resources, and models for examples as the essential ingredients in the change paradigm. The essential parts of a paradigm as defined in this book involve more comprehensive components of structure, thought, and process. Managers consistently evaluate the crises, leadership styles and abilities, infrastructures, visions and goals, outside resources, and successes of others. Unfortunately, the evaluations are temporary because these things change. It is critical to effective organizational change that assessment of conscious and unconscious issues are the more direct concerns of the evaluators and the change makers within organizations. The tried and true concerns of management are the ties that bind the organization to violence.

Balancing the human paradigm with the organizational history creates the existing organizational system. The process of the elimination of violence includes assessing the organizational history, the human history, and the outcome of change to create a new organizational paradigm devoid of violence. The next chapter provides a case example of an organization embracing its history and its future, thus creating change through nonviolence.

10

<hr>

Expunging Organizational Violence: A Case Study in Ethical Change

Building a system for eliminating organizational violence requires a consistent and congruent approach to holistic, ethical change. This chapter is a culmination of interventions with three clients. Chapters eight and nine focus on building the system with a step-by-step approach to expunging violence, which leads us to this chapter—a case study of three clients in varying stages of change. I have combined their stories into one case in an attempt to demonstrate how identification, planning, creating an aura of calm, and movement to ethical change can hold in check and inhibit the violence paradigm from being superimposed on the organizational paradigm.

It is critical to the overall understanding of this paradigm of violence that one recognize its varying parts as issues that block organizations from achieving success. Time is one factor that plagues organizations. We have become enamored with quick fixes and fast success. But quick fixes block organizations from embracing long-lasting change. In addition to time, permeations, or elements that weave throughout an entire process, are important in exploring and expunging violence from organizations pursuing strategies of change. This book suggests that one take the time to explore the incidents of life in an effort to create a holistic approach to balancing systems and people, rather than just cognitively discussing the issues of systems and people. Cognitive thinking is insufficient for expunging violence; experiencing the trauma allows one to actively pursue creating change. In other words, this book suggests that one not only stop and smell the roses, but one should spend time tending to the roses so that others may enjoy them as well.

The system for eliminating violence requires that balances within the existing organizational paradigm—human interaction, organizational history, objectives for change—exist to ensure that the organization identifies its underlying demon, the violence paradigm.

THE SITUATION

Bill is the chief administrative officer (CAO) of Southeast Center City and has held the position for two years. He is a young executive, having graduated from a prestigious university specializing in executive public government management. He moved to this city from the West Coast where he had been the executive in a city with a population over a million. His reputation has grown as a person who inspires and leads organizations into a new future. In fact, it was this reputation that paved the way for his ascension to his current job.

When Bill accepted his role, key problems were identified by the City Council. Rapid growth in housing and industry was creating changes at an alarming rate within the city. The city needed management that could maintain the city's cultural heritage and flavor of the Old South. The second critical problem facing the city was its changing demographics. An increasing number of African- and Latin-Americans had been moving into the city, making up 22 percent of the city's population. Based on this change, the council wanted to increase the ethnic ratio of the city's workforce. The third problem was the management style of the department directors. It appears that the fourteen department directors were heavy-handed in their approach to planning the scope of work. They made all the decisions, controlled all the information, usurped the hiring process, and ran their departments as fiefdoms. The council gave Bill three years to turn these problems around or the fourth year of his contract would be terminated.

Bill conducted an employee opinion survey with all 4,000 city employees. The results suggested that the issues raised by the council barely scraped the surface of the trouble brewing within the city. Being well-prepared, Bill determined that skills were needed beyond his own or those of his deputy manager and assistant manager to resolve the issues. Based on the results of Bill's Request for Proposal, a consultant was hired to accomplish all concerns stated within the request. The Request for Proposal stated the city's primary outcome:

the intervention planned for Southeast Center City must ensure that a balance is created between the needs of the employees, the council, and the Chief Administrative Officer that achieves the following: (1) increased ability of all affected parties to jointly function as a team to accomplish all council outcomes; (2) identifies and recommends alterations to any policies that negatively impact the directives of the council; and (3) builds a strategy for the future that ensures total quality management principles for the future and present.

The consultant upon review of the situation and in discussion with the CAO agreed to institute a process of change for the organization.

Bill is representative of many executives charged with creating change and managing major issues affecting the long-range future of their organizations. Bill's task is to craft a plan for leading the organization from past history into the creation of a new one. The challenges inherent in that charge often cause managers to make decisions that create the cycle of violence. Ineffective leaders begin to establish parameters of control in an attempt to move from point A to point B. The process created usually discounts the necessity to create effective bonds with employees; instead, the process focuses on power and authority as the guiding principles for movement. Bill is a positive model of change because he recognizes that time is an important factor in the overall success of the changes requested by the council. He spent the first two years of his administration developing relationships, assessing the balance between individual skills and teamwork, and listening to the solutions proposed by employees as well as their concerns. He works toward the concept of inclusion, and he realizes that a just end is required for the organization to be successful. In that process, however, he has recognized that fulfillment of the City Council's request requires a skilled professional who understands the process of change.

THE CONSULTANT'S PERSPECTIVE

The consultant meets with the CAO and is impressed with Bill's analysis of the issues. The consultant determines that the long history of the city is valued highly in the process. The council has stated that retaining the flavor of the Old South is a priority, including retention of old political strategies while creating changes below the level of CAO or Council.

The consultant is concerned that keeping the organization healthy might not allow preservation of the historical traditions. Change often alters the entire culture of an organization. Maintaining tradition might make it difficult for any real change to occur at all. The consultant develops a strategy for change that focuses on balancing the desired outcomes with keeping the existing organizational paradigm dominant over the violence paradigm. To be clear, the first step requires assessing time, resources, and scope of work needed to achieve the outcome. This is critical because unconscious issues of communication, decision making, collaboration, problem solving, and understanding of the systems in operation and what relationships had developed must be addressed in order for the organization to make movement. If it turns out that both conscious and unconscious issues are addressed before the request-for-proposal process, then the organization is on its way to success. If, however, the unconscious issues are overlooked, then the organization has to backtrack to ensure success.

In addition to these concerns, the consultant decides to define the structure guiding organizational decision making and to assess the congruence of the management of the organization with the council and the fourteen department directors. The consultant decides to utilize Lloyd C. Williams's Belief Systems Audit and Six Box Theory (*The Congruence of People and Organizations* [Westport, CT: Quorum Books, 1993]) as two points of analysis. If congruence exists, then the proposed intervention makes sense. If there is incongruence, then some analysis needs to occur to assess the driving force behind the desired change. Another instrument chosen for analysis is Kurt Lewin's Force Field Analysis (*Organizational Communication: The Essence of Effective Management* [Columbus, OH: Phillip Lewis Publishers, 1980]). The rationale for this instrument is to assess the readiness of the entire organization for change based on the existing organizational culture. Yet another analytical instrument is a review of all the existing vessels within the organization, which poses the questions: Is there a mission? Does the mission guide the development of guiding principles? Are there policies that create a standard within the organization for all types of actions, procedures, and practices? Can the operating procedures of the fourteen departments visibly reflect the policies and mission of the organization? Have the employees seen any of these items, or has the work been given to the employees in a piecemeal fashion suggesting that significant control factors are at play within the organization?

Upon answering these questions and completing the analysis, the consultant presents a realistic intervention strategy to the CAO. The consultant reviews the findings and determines that the organization is in need of intervention. The need is based on a lack of congruence between the organization's mission and policies, between its policies and procedures, and between procedures and the actual design of the work. The control factors within the organization also determine the need for intervention. There is a match between the skills of the consultant and the voids existent in organizational functioning, and an agreement is reached regarding the services to be rendered for Southeast Center City.

AUTHOR'S NOTE: Consultants are ethically bound to provide services to organizations based on real need. Too often, services are provided when they are not warranted, thereby creating an aura of chaos—the violence paradigm. It is important that organizations assess the efficacy of consultant usage based on real need, real analysis, and real data evaluation.

THE ORGANIZATIONAL FINDINGS

People Issues

Upon utilization of Williams's Six Box Theory, Belief Systems Audit, and Lewin's Force Field Analysis, the employees of the city stated that change had occurred throughout the city without warning and without including them in the change process. Management wanted things done their way or employees would face the consequences. Management also dictated the amount work to be done without regard to the employees' other assignments, suggesting that quantity of work was valued over quality. Employees also said that the new CAO was falling into the same behavioral patterns by discussing change without including the employees in the planning.

Based on these results, the consultant felt that it would be important to conduct a Trust Assessment (Jack Gibb, *Trust* [Los Angeles: Guild of Tutor Press, 1978]) to determine the degree of trust that existed within the organization. Upon conducting the assessment, the consultant discovered that the majority of operations within the organization were fear-based and within a circle of control. This meant that the organization was extremely top heavy in decision making and conflict resolution. The process of communication, development of relationships, collaboration, and system understanding were top-down processes. No valuing or validation of employees occurred. The consultant determined that change could not successfully occur without first addressing the tenets of violence. Working through the violence paradigm was critical to the successful changes envisioned by the CAO.

One of the principal problems identified by employees was the lack of inclusion. As a strategy for expunging the violence, the consultant and CAO agreed that openness was essential for employees to buy into the process. The process could also be aided by the CAO displaying vulnerability to the City Council in openly discussing the problems of the organization. With this in mind, a strategy of change was created.

The strategy encompassed:

1. identifying the issues existing within the organization;
2. reaching an agreement about balancing the desired outcome for the organization with creating wholeness within the organization;
3. establishing a framework for creating an aura of calm in order to address the issues that surfaced in the data analysis;
4. creating quality teams to ensure that the tenets and the structure of violence could be addressed as part an inclusion process;
5. embracing desired outcomes of the overall intervention by determining the degree of congruence between the existing organizational paradigm and the elements of the nonviolence paradigm; and
6. defining the areas within the organization that enhance continuation of circles of control versus circles of influence.

These agreed upon elements of a comprehensive strategy were the basis for discussion with employees and managers. Bill felt he understood all the issues involved in the proposed consultation. He discussed the strategy with the City Council and offered it as a model for retaining the city's Old South image while instituting change. They agreed that the process might be helpful.

The issues raised by the employees in their discussions with the consultant demonstrated the dynamics that occur in numerous organizations preparing for or implementing change. Management, not the organization, determined that existing conditions demand a change. In the case of this consultation, management needed to consider the health of the organization before embarking on a change strategy. Creating an aura of calm or a vacuum is essential to the organization in developing the ability to embrace organizational change. The imbalance of people issues to systems issues strongly dictates the need to focus on people issues and organizational violence before initiating systems change.

The other dynamic discovered in the consultation was that organizational problems existed before the plans for change were introduced. The organization's existing paradigm was threatened by the obvious discount of human resources. Service delivery to citizens was severely hampered by the styles of management within the fourteen departments. The desire to create change in the organization brought out the dysfunctional components of the organization and allowed management to confront them. Change opened the doors for exploration of the violence paradigm existing within the walls of the organization.

THE INTERVENTION PROCESS: LIVING WITH THE TENETS, STRUCTURE, AND PROCESS OF VIOLENCE

As the process being described is a systemic step-by-step approach, discussion throughout the intervention process focuses on the steps taken to expunge violence from the organization. Upon completion of the data analysis component of the intervention, the consultant met with all fourteen department directors, division-level staff, and managers. The first meeting was a learning meeting to describe the existing organizational paradigm and to describe the violence paradigm process. This was important because the employees were used to exclusion and secrecy as norms in the existing organizational paradigm. Opening up the communication process to end the secrecy was extremely helpful. Managers were able to share their own pain surrounding secrets and exclusion within the organization. This became the first opportunity for employees to discuss and to create bonds that had not existed previously. This process began the repairing of the tenets of violence that had long existed within the organization.

Five meetings were scheduled with all employees and their managers to begin the process of healing through the bonding process. At first, mistrust was the norm of the meetings, so the Afrocentric process of storytelling was used to stimulate the bonding process. Employees began to share their pain within the organization. Managers began to share their shame and their pain for participating in pushing employees away from each other and the management team. The process actually became a freeing experience for the participants. Three of the department directors felt the process was meaningless. They enjoyed their power and authority and felt that employees wanted too much from the organization. They also liked the policy of exclusion. However, the group began to value inclusion over exclusion. This was a significant step in the process; the bonding process was beginning and it strengthened the employees and managers to address the other tenets of violence.

Within a short period of time, the employees, managers, division chiefs, and department directors began to recognize a change in their interactions. The process of bonding opened the door to the unconscious assessments discussed earlier; the people of the organization began to focus on how they communicated, made decisions, resolved problems, collaborated in planning, developed relationships, and understood the system they had perpetuated. Referring back to Figure 7.3, the Six Box Theory includes the unconscious assessments that often get discounted in the development of change. The employees found themselves poised to make a dramatic shift in all the tenets of violence.

Simultaneous to this initial process of violence elimination, the city management staff and the City Council were busily defining the parameters of change that made sense for them. The struggle was in helping the council define its role in such a fashion that it did not usurp the authority it had placed in the chief administrative officer. This was a key point, because the council needed to understand that it consistently created violence in its relationship with the CAO. The violence was predicated on the consistent use of power and authority over the live-lihood of the CAO. Rather than creatively change the organization to achieve given outcomes of the council, the CAO was constantly bal-ancing what he believed needed to occur with the threat of doing too little in order to maintain his position within the organization. In their deliberations, members of council were able to state their fears of not being reelected. They had promised to maintain the flavor and traditions of the Old South in the community in spite of progress. The CAO stated that different persons see the traditions differently; therefore, the council did not need to carry the burden alone. Considering the options, they discussed that task forces, surveys, town meetings, and other strategies could be used to clarify the real needs of the citizenry. The council perceived this action on the part of the CAO as very different from its experience with past executive officers.

Some discussion occurred about the projections and the impact they had on the bonding among top decision makers. The process of ex-punging violence at the highest level had begun. The consultant's role in this process had become teacher and guide.

Changes were occurring in the rest of the organization as well. The tenets of violence, not the people, became the identified problems of the organization. Process was the problem, and the creation of a new process would be their savior.

Step two of the intervention involved addressing the vessels of vio-lence. As employees had lived under a cloud of fear, it was reasonable to assume that the vessels of violence—policies, procedures, and ad-ministrative regulations—were structured to control employees rather than influence them. Therefore, the process of violence and the vessels of violence were addressed simultaneously. As managers and employees talked about the desired outcomes of the management team and the council, they recognized that little attention had been given to standards that should guide how work was to be accomplished. The trick in the process was not to let the groups address all the issues at once. It was a tough task helping them remember all issues that must be addressed. This caused them to pull back and cross check all their findings and all their proposed changes. Each time a new issue arose, the team process (bonding, inclusion, embracing of their views) became stronger.

The council began to realize that it had not fulfilled its role to the employees. No standards existed within the organization to describe the philosophy or principles they believed should guide all action within the organization. The consultant worked with the CAO to enhance his skills in internal consultation. As his skills grew, he became the real staff to the council—being heard, being included, bonding stronger, oper-ating from influence instead of power, and realizing a true change in the operations of the top layer of the organization.

The employees began to question the role of the council and the CAO. They had not met yet in this process. In order to avoid the issue of open meeting laws, the council decided that each member would become a spokesperson to the different groups. Council members agreed upon the topics they would share, their philosophy, and the principles they wanted to guide the organization. They agreed to ask the employees for their final input prior to adopting the philosophy and principles at a council meeting. They were surprised that employees had thought about the organization, its strengths, and its weaknesses. The employees were surprised that the council was willing to talk with and listen to them and that they would seriously consider the opinions and advice of the employees. Again, the expunging process continued to expand as inclusion, bonding, embracing, and co-creating a just end became high values of the organization.

Every step toward expunging the tenets moved the violence paradigm to a lower level within the existing organizational paradigm. In fact, the existing organizational paradigm itself was shifting. Every consistent act by the politicians, executive management team, managers, and employees began to shift the organization. The aura of calm was being created and expanded by all parties within the organization. In terms of time, the intervention had now entered its third month.

The employees recognized that a new day was dawning on the organization. They discovered that management was becoming consistent, thereby increasing their trust in the process. The aura of calm was still intact, and the vacuum was allowing the employees to address the violence paradigm rather than the change originally expressed. What was not readily understood by the employees was the concept that addressing the violence, even crafting a new future around the violence, was providing them with new skills for dealing with the changes proposed by the council and executive management team. It is important to remember that no intrusion of change had occurred yet within the organization.

The council appointed task forces within the community. The council thus set the stage for bonding with citizens and including citizens in the process of change. The citizens seemed eager to participate in government. This suggests that controlling the citizenry is not needed. The council can share the parameters and boundaries that will help them create a strategy for changes to the community. The council members were surprised at the citizens' response to their call for inclusion. The citizens appeared surprised that they were asked. All in all, a sound, consistent process of inclusion and embracing ideas and ideals was emerging.

As all parties—employees, managers, executives, and citizens—gave input, the vessels of violence were being altered to fit the needs of all groups. Consistency and congruence became the watchwords for the changes occurring. Influence and the unconscious assessments became the process, and step three was beginning to emerge as the next phase of the process.

Step three involved addressing the structures of violence. The structures of violence are the absences of standards within the organization. It became evident to the employees and the managers that the lack of consistency contributed heavily to their feelings of violation. If the aura of calm was to continue beyond this intervention, then standards needed to be created that would give some guidance to employees about the way work was to be accomplished. This would also allow the employees to craft the manner in which the human resources of the organization would be led. The consultant helped the employees, managers, executives, and council members understand the concept of standards. Figure 10.1 repeats the four standards that guide organizations. These standards are created by different elements of the organization. The systems standard is created by the politicians in defining the philosophy and the principles of the organization, including the goal of the overall success of the city. The rules standards are created by the executive management team in the form of overriding policies and regulations that impact the success of the organization. These include personnel rules, civil service regulations, and the like. The department directors become accountable for the creation of organizational procedures and operational policies for day-to-day performance in adherence of the systems standard and the overriding rules standards. The managers and the employees are accountable for the appearance standard. The key to the appearance standard is ensuring congruence between the actions and words of the organization. The practice standards are created by employees in their everyday performance. Essential to effective practice standards are work habits and strategies that mirror the systems, rules, and appearance standards.

In this intervention, problems occurred when employees and managers began to look seriously at the rules, appearance, and practice standards. The risk occurred in the creation of rules that legislated behavior and thought too tightly. The quality teams began to experience old feelings of fear and control. The test of the evaporation of the tenets of violence was under serious scrutiny. The groups began to recognize that an aura of chaos was occurring. A new vacuum, stopping the actions altogether, was set in place. The employees revisited their experiences of bonding, inclusion, and embracing new views, ideas, and ideals. They rethought their experiences of influence versus control and collaboration versus power, authority, and control, and they revisited the structure of violence. They loosened the standards to ensure that the rules didn't result in power and control. They created examples for each rule stan-

Figure 10.1
Organizational Standards; Strategic Direction

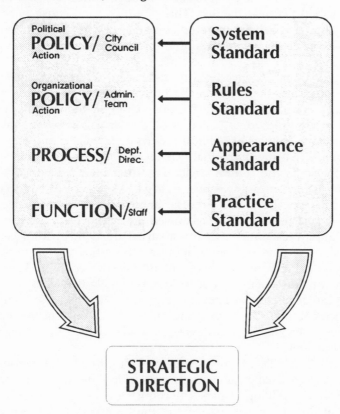

dard that could be demonstrated in the appearance and practice standards, and they worked harder as quality teams. They recreated the aura of calm.

The process of creating standards was an arduous one. Managers and employees decided that to be most effective, they would create the rules and appearance standards together. Herein lay real problems in the intervention. The management was used to creating policy, administrative regulations, procedures, and edicts regarding the way work was to be accomplished and the limits employees would experience. Employees only had experience following rules. Their lack of expertise caused them to continually look at strategies to create no rules to design a leaderless organization. After weeks of negotiations, a balance was achieved that had management creating the rules standards and employees designing simulations around the rules to see if an appearance standard could be accomplished that met the test. Three months later, consistency in the rules was accomplished, and employees felt that appearance standards were achievable—a happy ending to these components of the violence paradigm.

The process of violence was the next step. The process of violence focuses on interactions within the organization that take the path of influence or control. Southeast Center City experienced a consistent pattern of control circles, which created mistrust, miscommunication, inconsistency, feelings of political actions by managers and employees, and a sense that the individual was all that mattered. Teamwork was an anathema to the control circle. The trust that had begun to build throughout the process was now at stake. Management had to look at the outcomes of the control process. Immediately, some managers said that their mistrust of employees caused the employees to perform more work. Employees stated that the mistrust freed them from being accountable. The time and permeation factors of the control process had created an organizational history of disempowered staff. The disempowerment caused employees to lose key skills they had when they entered the organization. Lots of energy was expended discussing strategies focusing on trust, clear communication, competency-based work strategies, collaboration techniques, and we-oriented rather than I-oriented strategies.

The City Council's task forces were providing good information. However, they were asking for commitments from the council beyond what the council was willing to give. The council was asked to go on a retreat to look at the process of change and the trauma caused when organizational history is threatened. What the council had to realize was that two organizational histories were being rewritten simultaneously—that of the city organization and that of the council organization. The council had to confront its own organizational history and, therefore, its own violence paradigm. Tenets, vessels, structures, processes, and boundaries existed for the council just as they existed for the city organization. Thus, the council had to return to square one. They were no longer observers but participants, and the assumptions they made about citizens made them stakeholders in the expunging of violence. The members began to address the lack of bonding, inclusion, embracing, and influencing within the council itself. The hardest commitment that they had to make was working for the good of the organization and the council, not for their own personal good. The consultant helped them realize that their teamwork in creating real options for the city would ultimately benefit their individual political careers. To be successful, the

CAO had to assume the role of staff for them. Trust was the major barrier, yet it was the only savior. Three more months of hard work, and the trust relationship was growing.

We were now at the crossroads of expunging the violence paradigm. All the other components of the violence paradigm—tenets, vessels, structure, and process—were internally focused, and the boundaries of violence were externally driven. Balance of power, freedom of association, and incongruent competition strategies initiated and confronted the organizational history from external parameters. This means that although unions are a part of organizations, they exist outside of the organization by choice, with the purpose of making the organization conform to their wishes. The employees were stopped at this point. It had been a wonderful exercise helping to reshape the strategies, interactions, processes, and structure of the organization, but the employees now had to look at ending strategies they had created to protect themselves. How often we wished for change yet resist the change when it is at our doorstep. The employees wished for organizational inclusion; they got it. The employees wished for a better relationship with managers; they got it. The employees wanted to be heard; they were. Employees wanted the organization to shift toward influence rather than power, authority, and control; it did. The employees wanted just means to create just ends; they got it. Now they were confronted with eliminating the boundaries they created; could they give them up?

Through the intervention process, the employees could not give up the boundaries but could only alter them to test the effectiveness of the aura of calm. The employees entered into a Letter of Agreement with management that instituted many more informal rather than formal steps of resolution. They forced the management of the unions to accept their approach to creating change or they would decertify the unions. The employees requested that the associations initiate a moratorium on activity against the city for one year to test the success of the nonviolence paradigm. Phase one of the intervention was now complete; the aura of calm, the vacuum of change, had served its purpose.

Although this might have seemed like more than one phase, the entire intervention is really about creating change. Phase one was created to ensure that a balance existed for the rewriting of organizational history. In phase one, employees and managers learned strategies and techniques for embracing change and creating a new future. Now the employees and managers had to initiate the organizational change. The structure, vessels, tenets, processes, and boundaries were identified, planned for, and implemented prior to the initiation of a change process. Now the council, the city management team, the department directors, the managers, and the employees were all poised to embrace the change.

ORGANIZATIONAL CHANGE

The original request from the CAO of Southeast Center City was to help the organization shift from its existing organizational paradigm to a more inclusive paradigm. The three problems of the organization were: (1) the management style of the department directors; (2) changing demographics of the city and diversity inclusion; and (3) rapid growth. When the violence paradigm is expunged through a strategic response to the elements of that paradigm, the organization will be ready to look to address the changes it wants to make.

Management Style

Southest Center City consistently planned for change that would set the parameters for the intervention. Each change altered the approach of the department directors' management style. Specifically, each approach to creating standards, identifying rules, and establishing guiding principles framed the acceptable action of the department directors and the division managers. The ten-month process of expunging violence effectively altered the organizational history of the department directors and division managers.

Diversity Inclusion

The issue of diversity inclusion was a much larger issue for the organization. Expunging the tenets of violence effectively set the stage for the organization to embrace cultural differences. The CAO and the members of the City Council agreed to identify key reasons for the inclusion of minorities to the organizational structure. However, the consultant suggested that stating the key rationales for inclusion would not be sufficient. To truly embrace diversity, it was suggested that the members of the organization participate in awareness training to confront their own prejudices, which might affect the successful assimilation of ethnic diversity within the organization. Additionally, it was suggested that effective partnerships with the ethnic community could be built. To effectively manage the change, the minority churches, community centers, social action organizations, and special groups were contacted for their assistance in guiding organizational change. Focus groups were formed. A diversity training firm was contacted to assist in preparing the organization to embrace diversity. A three-pronged process of training, partnership building, and human resource recruiting efforts was identified as the strategy of choice. Over a six-month period, the training, creation of focus groups, partnership offerings and concentrated recruiting efforts were conducted based on parity data identified within the organization. The goal was to increase the minority employee staffing of Southeast Center City by 25 percent.

Rapid Growth in Southeast Center City

The issue of growth management balanced by maintaining traditional Southern values and customs was by far the hardest component of the intervention with Southeast Center City. The shift in industry, housing, demographics, education, tourism, transportation, service provisions, and economic and urban development was tantamount to the death of the Old South. The City Council was in many ways caught in the grip of progress. The advantage for the council was the inclusive process created ten months earlier in the task forces and focus groups created with the citizens. The key strategy for the city in embracing the changes was the building of effective partnerships with the business and social community.

The desired outcome of this growth management process was different from those faced by many other governments. The focus of growth management in this city was not housing or industry as is usually the case; instead, the growth management process focused on the ability of the community to embrace and include new values and ideas encompassing the new residents entering the community. The city legislature had established clear rules surrounding transportation, fiscal preparedness, land use rights, and the like. It was the community's responsibility, however, to prepare to integrate new perspectives into the ethos of the city. The council and focus groups decided that the chamber of commerce, the visitors and convention bureau, university leaders, and church leaders needed to meet with all new major businesses to impress upon them the values of the community and the changing face of the city. This allowed each new business to include in their relocation packages a value-added presentation of the new community. Addresses and names of key leaders from the majority and minority communities were contained in the relocation packages; key issues of the community were identified, and leaders responsible for embracing and creating new strategies were included so that newcomers could embrace their civic duties to participate in creating the change.

A total systems change involving organizational history was emerging. A balance had been created in the development of change for Southeast Center City. The city was in charge of its future, and the future looked very bright.

SUMMARY

This intervention was a huge success for the consultant. In my first book, *The Congruence of People and Organizations* (Westport, CT: Quorum

Books 1993), I describe a new approach to embracing unconditional management of human and organizational resources. This book identifies strategies of balancing organizational life with organizational pain. I used both sources successfully in this intervention. The three organizations from which this one story was condensed and for whom the consultations occurred are in different stages of creating nonviolence paradigms to guide their organizational maintenance and their organizational change.

What follows is a discussion of the nonviolence paradigm and what is required in the growth process.

11

Expunging Organizational Violence:
A Holistic Process

Critical to one's overall understanding of organizational violence is the ability to extricate oneself from the process long enough to survey the whole situation, which includes the comprehensive workings of an organization. Such is the case with surveying an organization's organizational history. Organizational history is the record, accumulated over time, that describes an organization's balanced or imbalanced approach to organizational movement and change. Every manager, director, executive, consultant, or politician should review the organizational history prior to considering change as a valid option for the organization.

To accomplish that feat, it becomes critical to recognize that an environment of balance and calm are key to understanding what exists within the organizational environment. Also, two assessments must occur simultaneously in surveying organizational history. Assessments of both the violence paradigm and the organizational paradigm are equally important for effective identification of organizational and personal issues. The underlying violence paradigm begins to dominate when discounting occurs within the organization. Consultants promote the violence paradigm when the neglect to pay attention to it. Executives and managers cause the violence paradigm to dominate because they do not balance the tenets of violence with any other organizational issue. Employees cause the violence paradigm to move based on their reactions to feeling discounted or controlled, which usually results in the creation of boundaries of violence. Politicians cause the violence paradigm to move because of their I-oriented approach to change. Irrespective of one's preference, expunging violence is based on collaboratively planned approaches to maintenance or change. To be self-directed or self-styled impedes real change and real maintenance.

The primary cause of the superimposition of violence becomes planning incrementally, or planning without assessing the balance factors of the organization. Organizational leaders often assess a given issue based on the change that is proposed or the problem that has arisen. Unfortunately, time or the lack of time becomes the issue that often guides the planning. When time is short, planning occurs for the specific issue without an assessment of how the plan affects other areas of the organization. The second cause of the superimposition of the violence paradigm is overlooking or discounting the impact of the plan on issues of bonding, inclusion, influence, and the embracing of ideas that are critical to employees. When time is short, it is often believed that those issues can be dealt with later, which rarely occurs. The third factor is more insidious, that it's just not important to worry about the issues of bonding, inclusion, influence, embracing of ideas, or creating just ends—that the employees will fall in line of their own accord. Each factor is a part of the dynamic of creating organizational violence.

The issue for consideration is a holistic approach to expunging violence. In the previous chapters, we have looked at a step-by-step approach, and we have explored a case where expunging violence was critical to the development of realistic change to organizational history. Leaving the discussion at that point evades the global view.

The global view of organizational violence is illustrated in Figure 11.1. It is composed of three phases. Phase one focuses on the impetus that begins the movement of the violence paradigm from a coexistent place to a primary place in the life of the organization. An issue suggesting change, a problem impacting the entire organization, and the acquisition of new senior management are all examples of stimuli that can trigger the organizational violence process. When the process is triggered, phase two commences.

Phase two starts with the initiation of pain or trauma. Employees feel trapped and hurt, and they try to find ways to understand and deal with these feelings. In the process, they confront management in order to gain understanding. This usually initiates dysfunctional communication. The dysfunctional communication cycle sets up the initiation of the circle of control versus the circle of influence. When there is lack of balanced resolution in the dysfunctional communication cycle, the violence paradigm begins to superimpose itself on the existing organizational paradigm. Thus, the external forces to the organizational paradigm become dysfunctional communication and control. Phase two can take months to occur, but when unchecked, years can pass before the organization recognizes that violence is the real issue that permeates the

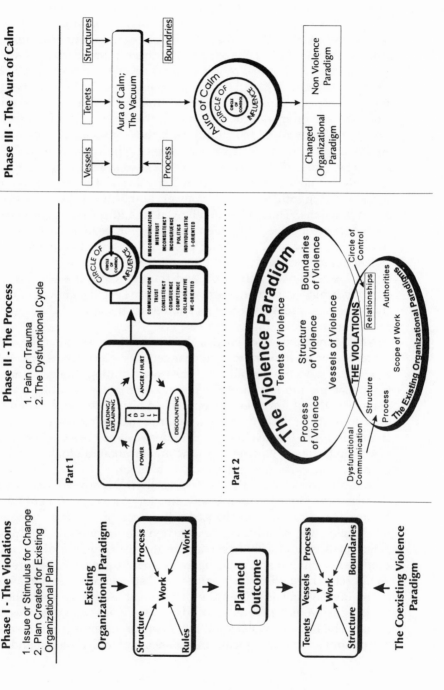

Figure 11.1
Global View of Organizational Violence

organization. Lack of effective time utilization and permeations of control, mistrust, incompetence, politics, and I-orientation create a monstrous violence paradigm that governs the work and the people.

Phase three begins the process of expunging the violence. The first issue is the creation of an aura of calm or organizational vacuum. This process requires that management step back from changes to organizational structures, rules, processes, and people to ensure that healing can begin to occur. Without the calm, constant uproar becomes the status quo, which the organization comes to trusts. When the aura of calm is established, then management can look at each element of the violence paradigm. This means that the organization must make time to work on the tenets of violence. Bonding, balancing individuation with team, creating an aura of inclusion versus exclusion, embracing versus discounting employee ideas and ideals, creating just means to just ends and embracing influence versus power, authority, and control become the first actions. Time must be allowed to address *each* component of the tenets of violence. Only then should action be taken to address the vessels, structure, and process of violence. It is crucial to remember that violence continues because we often overlook one or more components in our haste to rectify the pain and trauma. Once the process of expunging begins, consistency and congruence keep the aura of calm alive and strong. Inconsistency breeds and festers the aura of chaos and uproar becomes the operative process.

When consistent work creates the healing process, then the organization can begin to work toward change. This is a collaborative system. A new executive must build bonds before instituting change; a manager must examine the health of the organization before creating a change to the way things have been accomplished historically; and an employee must look at the desired outcome prior to instituting balance-of-power strategies. Once the healing is well underway and once the nonviolence paradigm begins to emerge, then the organization can look at strategies to change the existing organizational paradigm.

I recently consulted with a business activity department of a city government. The city had hired a new director of this department the year before. The director was charged with creating massive change that would allow the organization to function more smoothly. The director determined very quickly in his tenure that a restructure of the organization was required and a management analyst needed to be hired who would act as his advisor on organizational structural issues and as coach to the division chiefs within the department. Although the actions of the director were structurally sound, the outcomes were much less than sound. The director violated all the tenets of violence from the outset. No attempt at bonding, inclusion, balancing of individuation and team, embracing of employees and division chiefs views, establishing just ends, or operating from influence versus power, authority, and control were considered by the new director. The director's actions in effect forced the superimposition of the violence paradigm on his department. When the director was confronted by the division chiefs and the employees, the director became entrenched in his perspective that he was the boss and controlled the outcomes of the department.

The resultant behavior was the initiation of phase two. The employees experienced the dysfunctional communication cycle and the circle of control. Employees totally mistrusted the actions of the director. Employees experienced miscommunication, and they believed the director was incompetent because he had not taken the time to understand the existing organizational history and the existing codes. Employees found the director to be inconsistent, and they felt that politics guided the process. There was some truth to this belief as the deputy city manager informed all management that the director was here to stay, and should they be unable to fall in line, they would need to leave.

The rules and vessels of the organization became more unclear, often creating an even stronger feeling of violence. Standards—the structures of violence—appeared to change daily. Employees felt discounted, abused, and misunderstood, and so did the director. A system impasse had occurred.

The process initiated by the director was unintentional. The director firmly believed that his approach to change was an appropriate one, albeit that employees felt violated. He believed that the employees had not given his approach a chance. The tenets of violence had been violated because they were not considered important in the planning process. The violence paradigm was not considered an equal partner to the organizational paradigm. Whenever unintentional arrogance guides organizational action, the violence paradigm rears its head and begins the process of superimposition.

To alter the process, the director had to create an aura of calm. Calm is created when employees understand that no change will occur until the tenets, vessels, structure, process, and boundaries of violence are addressed by the organization. In this case, the director had to return to square one and attend to the history, needs, aspirations, and fears of the employees. If the goal was a changed organizational paradigm and a nonviolent paradigm, then change must occur as a comprehensive process based on collaboration, clear communication, consistent performance, and a we-oriented approach to organizational change and maintenance.

The process of intervention focused on healing and of the circle of influence. Throughout the intervention, consistency was highly valued.

The moment inconsistency occurred, healing retreated to a lower level, requiring a more concerted effort to bring it to the forefront. Balance and calm were again the watchwords for successful change.

The preceding discussion involves the structural concern for the global view of organizational violence. Change agents, executives, politicians, managers, and employees are all accountable for the healing and the movement within an organizational paradigm as well as for the accuracy of the work scope changes essential to rewrite organizational history. Success is based on the ability of leaders to rise above the specific issues to survey the whole situation and create new bridges for success. Building bridges requires a balancing of people issues and system issues, recognizing that simultaneous intervention is required for creating a new paradigm. This is the challenge in the global, holistic view of organizational violence.

Too much of work within organizations is disjointed. As a consequence, too much of the interaction within organizations is contrived, and too much of the work within organizations needs to be redone. As I developed this system, it became apparent to me that each of these factors contributes to a compartmentalized organizational history. Although organizational history can never be eradicated, everyone can help shape history in such a fashion that it provides for a well-planned, holistic future. That is the rationale surrounding the development of a process to expunge organizational violence. Only through a global, holistic assessment can change occur that balances people and organizations.

12

The Nonviolence Paradigm: Explanations of Our Growth

This book focuses on the creation of balance and wholeness through expunging the violence paradigm, which is critical to the successful maintenance or growth of an organizational paradigm. This chapter looks at growth through the eyes of the consultant. I have witnessed the lack of balance and wholeness in governments, private corporations, and not-for-profit organizations. In each case, leaders and decision makers of organizations have focused on a specific issue or an identified problem within the organization or the political intrusion of the organization. In all of the cases, the co-existent violence paradigm moved from a sublevel to the primary focus of the organization. Almost unanimously, the leaders and decision makers shifted to a blame-and-shame mode where an issue, problem, employee, external group, or politician was blamed for the dysfunction identified at the moment. Rarely did the leader recognize the pattern of pain and trauma created within the organizational history of the corporation or government. Figure 12.1 depicts the two end points of organizational, and to some degree personal, systems that make the transition from pain and trauma to wholeness. In the diagram, all components of the system exist within a loose boundary at one end of the spectrum, while all components but one exist within a tighter boundary at the other end of the spectrum. The two ends of the spectrum display the real issues of violence and nonviolence.

Growth is possible whenever a *balance* exists within personal or organizational life. Whenever thoughts, beliefs, or actions are tightly struc-

Figure 12.1
Growth/Nongrowth

Growth

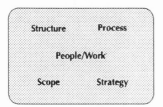

Nongrowth

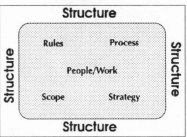

tured, one feels pressured, constricted, or out of control—out of balance. The dynamics of organizational history mirror personal or professional experiences around growth and movement. People and systems need to be interrelated with each other. Systems (with an organizational history) do not fare very well when its members are denied or discounted. Neither do people (with a personal history) fare very well when the organizational system is denied or discounted. This is what tries to illustrate.

The primary component or element that allows balance to occur is the aura of calm. As long as chaos exists, it is difficult to step back and depersonalize the experiences to discover the driving elements of calm. In the various examples throughout the book, the aura of calm is important because it allows people and organizations to focus on healing the tenets of violence. The aura of calm allows people and organizations to examine the vessels of violence with particular attention to the congruence factors of the vessels, and to examine the existence or nonexistence of standards with a keen eye toward the creation of reasonable and achievable standards. From an aura of calm, people and organizations can embrace the process of violence. People and organizations are able to confront interacting and changing events through control or influence. The aura of calm also allows people and organizations to mutually win rather than lose. Balance-of-power, freedom of association, and incongruent competition strategies are the elements of mutual loss. Traditional organizations unknowingly create strategies for mutual loss by their actions and by blaming others. Growth and wholeness is based on mutual winning and creating balance.

The left side of Figure 12.1 shows all components of a healthy growth system, which represents both organizations and individuals. Regardless of what type of system it represents, however, growth is based on the balance. In this figure, structure, process, scope, and strategy are the balanced components of the system so people within the system can allow changes or maintenance of the system to remain in perspective. All components of the system are equal, so there is mutual winning. Structure, process, scope of maintenance or change, and strategy exist only to support the other components of the system. People remain whole because the balance is attainable.

The converse can be seen on the righthand side of the figure. A new dimension—rules—is added to the system because more rigid boundaries are in existence. The boundaries are governed by structure, so no change occurs if it abuts the structure. On the left side of the figure, there is no sense that boundaries are static or unchangeable. On the right side, the boundaries are clearly defined, creating enormous difficulty for persons or systems to experience movement. The rigidness of the boundaries traps people and organizations into the violence paradigm. The left side is a freer moving process because it encompasses the nonviolence paradigm.

The outcome for all people and systems is to improve or enhance what has been occurring historically. If nongrowth is the outcome because of the violence paradigm, then people and systems become more restrictive toward achieving any goals. Energy is focused on protection and stability. If growth is the outcome because of the nonviolence paradigm, then people and systems become more relaxed, more engaging, and more embracing in achieving goals. Energy can then be focused on awareness and change that works toward overall outcomes.

It is important that we rethink the process of interacting with others and how the process of changing and growing is directly tied to the balance we create in working with each other and working with the issues of change. Our challenge is creating balance and recognizing the violence we create, expunging it by allowing the systems to come into balance. The aura of calm or the vacuum is a marvelous tool for creating balance. The rethinking of our histories to create a future is a constant struggle. Embracing all issues, not just some, is the strategy for balance.

Appendix

Assessing Organizational Violence

ASSESSING ORGANIZATIONAL VIOLENCE

Recognizing Your Organization's Role in Trauma

Following is an instrument for discovering organizational violence. The instrument is not designed to assess value or blame for internal organizational action; rather the instrument allows the organization to identify areas of imbalance that impact successful organizational life. Please rank your answers to each statement TRUE or FALSE using corresponding column.

A. Members of the organization believe that relationships within the organization are:

TRUE FALSE

1. _____ _____   Easy to make.

2. _____ _____   Predominately based on open communication.

3. _____ _____   Founded on trust.

4. _____ _____   Meeting the needs of the members because of clear
                   expectations.

5. _____ _____   Based on power that has been established by the leaders.

TRUE FALSE

6. _____ _____   Based on influence that has been established by the leaders.

7. _____ _____   Based on Control that has been established by the leaders.

8. _____ _____   Not meeting the needs of the members because of unclear

expectations.

9. _____ _____   Examples of effective sharing and caring among people who

become a part of the organization.

10. _____ _____   Hard to make.

B. People who do well in this organization tend to:

TRUE FALSE

1. _____ _____   Explicitly follow the rules.

2. _____ _____   Walk over every one else.

3. _____ _____   Speak their mind and get rewarded for it.

4. _____ _____   Make no decisions.

5. _____ _____   Challenge the rationale for the actions of the organization.

6. _____ _____   Remain silent and foster the status quo.

7. _____ _____   Understand   the   standards   required   for   effective

Performance.

TRUE FALSE

8. _____ _____   Make the standards for effective performance as the situation arises.

9. _____ _____   Operate from a stance of controlling everything in the work.

10. _____ _____   Operate from a stance of influencing everyone involved in the work.

C. The organization treats its members as:

TRUE FALSE

1. _____ _____ Laborers

2. _____ _____ Partners

3. _____ _____ Co-creators

4. _____ _____ Slaves

5. _____ _____ Associates

TRUE FALSE

6. _____ _____ Friends

7. _____ _____ Family

8. _____ _____ Employees

9. _____ _____ Stakeholders

10 _____ _____ Entrepreneurs

D. People are managed, directed, influenced, shaped within the organization by:

TRUE FALSE

1. _____ _____   People in positions of authority who use power to get things to happen.

2. _____ _____   People in positions of authority who use influence to involve others in getting things to happen.

3. _____ _____   The systems, rules, procedures and policies that shape what people should do.

4. _____ _____   The whims of management because the system, rules, procedures and policies change too much to shape what people do.

5. _____ _____   Their sense of commitment to the nature of the work and the organization.

6. _____ _____   Their sense of fear regarding the rewards and punishments of the organization.

7. _____ _____   The styles of the supervisors.

8. _____ _____   The styles of the co-workers.

9. _____ _____   The influence of the Union Activity.

10 _____ _____   The standards of the organization for work.

E. Relationships between co workers is usually:

TRUE FALSE

1. _____ _____   Competitive

2. _____ _____   Collaborative

3. _____ _____   Influential

4. _____ _____   Overt and above board.

5. _____ _____   Trusting

6. _____ _____   Based on Competence

7. _____ _____   An expectation of the organization to accomplish the
                  work.

8. _____ _____   Cooperative

9. _____ _____   Friendly

10 _____ _____   Indifferent

F.   Based on the relationship you described, please share what would help you
      have a better relationship.

TRUE FALSE

1. _____ _____   More Time for Clarification of roles

2. _____ _____   More time for identifying outcomes

TRUE FALSE

3. _____ _____   Nothing, I don't want anymore contact

4. _____ _____   Less time for clarification of roles

5. _____ _____   Less time for identifying outcomes

G.   When I think of my supervisor, I feel

TRUE FALSE

1. _____ _____   Good about the interaction

2. _____ _____   Afraid of the outcome of the interaction

3. _____ _____   Excited about the new assignment

4. _____ _____   Controlled by the interaction

5. _____ _____   Unsure of the conversation

H.   When I think of my coworkers, I feel

TRUE FALSE

1. _____ _____   Good about the interaction

2. _____ _____   Afraid of the outcome of the interaction

3. _____ _____   Excited about the new assignment

4. _____ _____   Controlled by the interaction

TRUE FALSE

5. _____ _____   Unsure of the conversation

I. _____ _____   The organization has clear rules.

J. _____ _____   The organization has clear policies.

K. _____ _____   I believe that the organization is fair in the application of

the rules

L. _____ _____   I believe that the organization is too complicated

M. _____ _____   The organization has no standards for performance.

N. _____ _____   Standards are a process of controlling employees.

O. _____ _____   Standards are helpful in my experiencing equitable

treatment.

P. _____ _____   This organization includes me in decisions affecting my job.

Q. _____ _____   This organization values competent work.

R. _____ _____   This organization values teamwork.

S. _____ _____   Getting things accomplished as a unit is a high value.

T. _____ _____   I feel that I must protect myself on the job.

U. _____ _____   I like my job and feel that I am respected.

TRUE FALSE

V. _____ _____ The organization provides training opportunities to ensure that I am well prepared to perform my job.

W. _____ _____ I can talk with my supervisor when I have a problem and know that the supervisor will assist me in achieving a resolution to the problem.

X. _____ _____ I can talk with my coworkers when I have a problem and know that my coworkers will assist me in achieving a resolution to the problem.

Y. _____ _____ I can be creative in my job to achieve different outcomes and trust that my efforts will be appreciated and recognized.

Z. _____ _____ I am in charge of how far I can progress within the organization.

ASSESSING ORGANIZATIONAL VIOLENCE

TABULATING YOUR RESULTS

Following is a tabulation sheet for assessing your Organizational Violence Score. Please mark your answers to the instrument on these sheets and tabulate the score. A "t" by the number means TRUE. A "f" by the number means FALSE.

OV Answers		OW Answers	
A1 f____	B1 t____	A1 t____	B1 f____
A2 f____	B2 t____	A2 t____	B2 f____
A3 f____	B3 f____	A3 t____	B3 t____
A4 f____	B4 t____	A4 t____	B4 f____
A5 t____	B5 f____	A5 f____	B5 t____
A6 f____	B6 t____	A6 t____	B6 f____
A7 t____	B7 f____	A7 f____	B7 t____
A8 t____	B8 t____	A8 f____	B8 f____
A9 f____	B9 t____	A9 t____	B9 f____
A10 t____	B10 f____	A10 f____	B10 t____

OV Answers   OW Answers

C1 t_____   D6 t_____   C1 f_____   D6 f_____

C2 f_____   D7 t_____   C2 t_____   D7 f_____

C3 f_____   D8 t_____   C3 t_____   D8 f_____

C4 t_____   D9 t_____   C4 f_____   D9 f_____

C5 f_____   D10 f_____   C5 t_____   D10 t_____

C6 f_____   E1 t_____   C6 t_____   E1 f_____

C7 t_____   E2 f_____   C7 f_____   E2 t_____

C8 f_____   E3 f_____   C8 t_____   E3 t_____

C9 f_____   E4 f_____   C9 t_____   E4 t_____

C10 f_____   E5 f_____   C10 t_____   E5 t_____

D1 t_____   E6 f_____   D1 f_____   E6 t_____

D2 f_____   E7 f_____   D2 t_____   E7 t_____

D3 f_____   E8 f_____   D3 t_____   E8 t_____

D4 t_____   E9 f_____   D4 f_____   E9 t_____

D5 f_____   E10 t_____   D5 t_____   E10 f_____

Appendix

OV Answers

OW Answers

F1 f_____   K f_____   F1 t_____   K t_____

F2 f_____   L t_____   F2 t_____   L f_____

F3 t_____   M t_____   F3 f_____   M f_____

F4 t_____   N t_____   F4 f_____   N f_____

F5 t_____   O f_____   F5 f_____   O t_____

G1 f_____   P f_____   G1 t_____   P t_____

G2 t_____   Q f_____   G2 f_____   Q t_____

G3 f_____   R f_____   G3 t_____   R t_____

G4 t_____   S f_____   G4 f_____   S t_____

G5 t_____   T t_____   G5 f_____   T f_____

H1 f_____   U f_____   H1 t_____   U t_____

H2 t_____   V f_____   H2 f_____   V t_____

H3 f_____   W f_____   H3 t_____   W t_____

H4 t_____   X f_____   H4 f_____   X t_____

H5 t_____   Y f_____   H5 f_____   Y t_____

I f_____   Z f_____   I t_____   Z t_____

J f_____   J t_____

OV Answers   OW Answers

Score   Score

_____   _____

Subtract your OW Answers Score from your OV Answers Score

to obtain your Violence Score

OV_____ - OW_____ = _____OVI

UNDERSTANDING THE ORGANIZATIONAL VIOLENCE ASSESSMENT

The purpose of the instrument is to give you some idea of the organizational health of your company. Each question or statement has been formulated to allow you to project what you believe occurs within your organization. Your perception often guides your actions; therefore, your perception of actions, thoughts, rules, and policies within your organization guides your overall assessment of the workplace. The instrument allows you to identify and quantify your organizational health.

When you tally your score, subtracting the organizational wellness (OW) score from the organizational violence (OV) score, you identify your *organizational violence index*. Scores on the violence index can be both positive and negative. The larger the violence index, the more unhealthy the organization; the smaller the violence index, the healthier the organization.

ORGANIZATIONAL VIOLENCE INDEX

A range of scores indicates which factors of the organization need attending to.

Positive Score Ranges

0 to 5	The organization is healthy, but strain is beginning to occur in the tenets of violence. It is important to assess relationships, bonding, inclusiveness, and ability of the organization to hear and respond to differences and diversity.
6 to 10	Relationships within the organization are at a low ebb. Supervision, practices of the organization, and the vessels (rules, policies, and procedures) are unclear, creating stress and opening the gates for organizational dysfunction.
11 to 20	The organization is devoid of clear, measurable, and manageable standards. Politics appears to guide organizational action, and the stance of employees and managers is to protect themselves from the actions of co-workers, supervisors, and managers.
21 and above	The organization is violent. Standards are out of line. The organization appears to operate from a circle of control rather than a circle of influence. Employees band together and utilize the resources of unions and associations to balance the power of the organization.

Negative Score Ranges

0 to −5	The organization is fairly healthy. However, some attention is required in evaluating the effectiveness of relationships within the organization and the congruence of the vessels of the organization.
−6 to −20	The organization is healthy, yet a sound balance between the tenets and vessels of violence with the structure and process of violence needs to be insured.
−21 and above	The organization is moving forward and needs to document its success, paying attention to ensuring continued health and prosperity.

Bibliographic Essay

Throughout the development of this book, numerous theorists were critical to my developing a framework for addressing the issue of organizational violence. Some of the theorists were important for background research, some of the theorists were cited as critical to my thinking in the actual writing of the book, and others were critical to my development of the instrument for assessing organizational violence as a starting point.

The following theorists were surveyed as background for developing a theory of organizational violence: M. Zenley, *Autopoiesis: A Theory of the Living Organization* (New York: North Holland, 1981); A. Woodcock and M. Davis, *Catastrophe Theory* (New York: Dutton, 1978); J. G. Miller, *Living Systems* (New York: McGraw-Hill, 1978); J. P. van Gigch, *Applied General Systems Theory* (New York: Harper & Row, 1974); D. M. Jamieson et al., ed., *The General Theory of Systems Applied to Management and Organizations* (Seaside, CA: Intersystems Publications, 1980); and G. Burrell and G. Morgan, *Sociological Paradigms and Organizational Analysis* (Englewood Cliffs, NJ: Prentice-Hall, Inc., 1979). Each of these theorists was influential in helping me develop a comprehensive approach to organizational analysis, sociological intent, and theoretical development.

Other theorists were essential in balancing the organizational sociological process with the psychodynamic intention evident in all organizations. These theorists were: M. Buber, *I and Thou* (New York: Scribner, 1970); V. Frankl, *Man's Search for Meaning* (Boston: Beacon Press, 1963); R. D. Laing, *The Politics of Experience* (New York: Pantheon, 1967); Pierre Teilhard de Chardin, *The Future of Man* (New York: Harper, 1969); P. Tillich, *The Courage to Be* (New Haven, CT: Yale University Press, 1980); and R. Assagioli, *Psychosynthesis* (New York: Penguin Press, 1976).

A. J. Muste, "The Situation and Program of Christianity," *Religion in Life* 8

(1939), pp. 223–224, was essential in assessing the relationship of human beings and their relationships. Lloyd C. Williams, *The Congruence of People and Organizations: Healing Dysfunction from the Inside Out* (Westport, CT: Quorum Books, 1993), provided theories of congruence, balance, and belief structures central to a comprehensive approach to organizational and systems change. James Cone, *Liberation* (Philadelphia: J.P. Lippincott Company, 1970) was helpful in addressing the issue of effective policy and its impact on freedom and the development of nonviolence. Gabriel Vahanian, *The Death of God* (New York: Braziller, 1961) was critical to my understanding of adjustment failure and the concepts of psychodynamic and social theorists. Irving Janis, *Victims of Groupthink* (Boston: Houghton Mifflin, 1972), was extremely effective in addressing the illusions of invulnerability often prevalent in organizations. Jack Gibb, *Trust: A New View of Personal and Organizational Development* (Los Angeles: Guild of Tutor Press, 1978), was essential in defining defending practices that occur for individuals and organizational systems. Peter Berger, *Invitation to Sociology: A Humanistic Perspective* (Garden City, NY: Doubleday, 1963), helped me develop the concept of the aura of calm. His approach to movement from one span of history to another was most enlightening in the development of organizational historical movement. David Osborne and Ted Gaebler, *Reinventing Government* (Reading, MA: Addison-Wesley, 1992), helped in developing factors of fundamental change. All of these authors' ideas were blended together to form my organizational violence theory.

Finally, many instruments were essential in the consultation with all of the organizations who were clients for the creation and implementation of this theory. Marvin Weisbord's Six Box Organizational Analysis (*Organizational Behavior: An Applied Psychological Approach* [Dallas: Hammer and Organ, 1978]) was essential to understanding overall organizational dynamics. Kurt Lewin's Force Field Analysis (*Organizational Communication: The Essence of Effective Management*, 2nd ed. [Columbus, OH: Phillip Lewis Grid Publishers, 1980]) was very helpful in assessing the readiness of organizations to embrace change. Lloyd C Williams's Belief Systems Audit and Six Box Process (in *The Congruence of People and Organizations* [Westport, CT: Quorum Books, 1993]) were very helpful in defining the internal structure of organizational process and history. Jack Gibb's Defending Process significantly guided my thinking on roles created within organizations.

The blending of all these readings has made this a richer system, for it encompasses psychology, theology, sociology, management theory, and new Afrocentrist and Eurocentrist thought.

Index

About the Author

LLOYD C. WILLIAMS is President of Lloyd C. Williams & Associates and Human Resources Manager of Employee and Organizational Development for the City of Las Vegas. He has consulted for governments and private organizations, including the states of Washington, Oregon, California, Arizona, Alabama, and Nevada; numerous city and county governments; academic institutions; health institutions; and private corporations.